MW00900083

Common Sense

When and if you busy guys
can find time — I feel sure
you will find this interesting.

May 17, 2005

Common Sense

❖

the #1 Critical Success Factor

It's Not Rocket Science

Edwin M. Glasscock, Ph.D.

iUniverse, Inc.
New York Lincoln Shanghai

Common Sense
the #1 Critical Success Factor

iUniverse books may be ordered through booksellers or by contacting:

iUniverse
2021 Pine Lake Road, Suite 100
Lincoln, NE 68512
www.iuniverse.com
1-800-Authors (1-800-288-4677)

ISBN: 0-595-33415-6 (pbk)
ISBN: 0-595-66910-7 (cloth)

Printed in the United States of America

This book is dedicated to—

First and foremost, this book is dedicated to my family…Mariben, Jenna, Tom and Tom's wife, Ellen Fraker-Glassscock.

It is also dedicated to men I have helped who also helped me. Over periods ranging from fifteen to thirty years, I have worked on a variety of management problems with everyone on this list.

Husel Ekaireb, Member of the Board of Directors, Merck & Co.

Henry Gadsden, Chairman and CEO, Merck & Co.

Ron Gelbman, Worldwide Chairman, Pharmaceutical & Diagnostics Group, Johnson & Johnson

Jim Hascall, Chairman and CEO, PRIMEX Technologies

Jim Latendresse, Director of Human Resources, Merck & Co.

Lewis Sarett, Ph.D., Senior Vice President, Science and Technology, Merck & Co.

Ajit Shetty, Ph.D., Chairman, Janssen Pharmaceutica, N.V.

Jim Towey, Chairman and CEO, Olin Corporation

Bill Weldon, Chairman and CEO, Johnson & Johnson

Verne Willaman, Member Executive Committee, Johnson & Johnson

Bob Wilson, Senior Vice Chairman, Board of Directors, Johnson & Johnson

John Winters, Vice President, Caterpillar Inc.

Contents

Comments from Readers

In the process of writing this book, I first sent individual chapters, then sections then the entire manuscript to various people. I was seeking constructive criticisms and got testimonials. These are some of the comments.

"The thing that I enjoyed most was the fact that these chapters contain such practical and applicable points. I think the insights in your book are incredibly valuable."

"This book is a real eye-opener! Hundreds of "how-to-succeed" volumes go on and on about what almost always turns out to be "small stuff". It's a masterpiece and belongs in every executive's library."

"I found your book be a very interesting and a fast, easy read. It gives readers a lot of very practical advice on how to improve their effectiveness: not just in their careers, but also in their personal lives. I think every manager would benefit from your sage advice."

"This book is as brilliant as it is simple: we need to think before we act. And you're right, 'It's not rocket science.' You set up a framework throughout the book that forces us to question our objectives."

"I can't tell you how much I enjoyed reading the manuscript. Thankfully, I was afforded the opportunity to read it in one setting, during a flight to Denver, and, although I was very tired during this trip, I didn't want to stop reading."

"The piece on leverage is one of the best articles I have ever read in management literature."

"I love your point that says judgment is the process of making choices. Your examples paint an excellent picture that I believe the reader can identify with. You give some very good guidelines for decision-making."

"People in all walks of life whether they are homemakers or business executives can profit from the ideas you explain so well. It is clear, straightforward, well organized, persuasive, and really holds your attention."

"I recently attended a conference, and at this conference I received four of the recent best sellers in management. I skimmed through them. They did not hold my interest. Most of what they talked about had been said before. I found your material really held my attention it was hard to put down. I like the stories, and I learned a great deal."

"The text is well written, easy to follow, and complimented greatly by the real world case studies and scenarios. The writing is smooth and almost feels like an actual conversation—one with a great communicator. The thing that I enjoyed most was the fact that these chapters contain such practical and applicable points."

"Many business texts attempt to introduce new, complicated, difficult to remember concepts that are suppose to enhance or support one's leadership qualities. Your book is one of the most practical ones I have ever read, and can apply to almost anyone in the professional world, irrespective of their current rank or title. If someone has aspirations for success, they will learn some very valid and simple tips from your book that will enhance their chances for success."

What This Book Is All About

This is a book for and about successful people.

Are you one of them? Clearly, you are—or have aspirations to be—if you are taking the time to read this book.

What is success and what does it take to achieve it?

> *Successful people are able to achieve superior results and a superior reputation while building strong relationships. In these three respects, they surpass others in their peer group.*

The 3 *R*'s of Success

Results

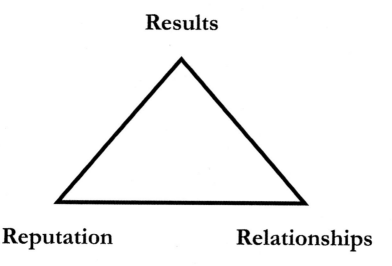

Reputation   Relationships

We are defining successful individuals as people who:

1. Achieve superior results.

2.   Earn a favorable reputation.

3.   Develop a network of relationships that makes them stand out in their peer group.

Several points need to be made about the three R's model. It should be clear that these are inextricably linked with each other. For example, you can achieve superior results, in part, because of relationships you have established. Or, you have a good reputation because of the results you have achieved.

The relative weight of each of the three R's varies. It can depend on the culture. In a political oriented company or a family controlled business, relationships become paramount. Conversely, in first-rate companies, results are most important. The relative weight of each also depends on circumstances. For example, if there are three candidates for a job opening and all have achieved outstanding results, reputation and relationships will determine the outcome.

Our definition is quite different from the conventional view in the management literature which defines success in terms of the position one has in a hierarchy. Let me use military organizations to illustrate this point. A general might command 10,000 troops. If we define success hierarchically, the successful people in this group are at the top or near the top of some pyramid; in this case maybe 10 high level officers. How about the other 9,990? **By our definition, any individual at any level in the organization can be successful**. For example, a sergeant who, compared to other sergeants, measures up well in terms of the three R's is a success. Conversely, even though he had a big job, a general might not be successful when we use his peers as the yardstick. It is possible to have first-class corporals and fourth-class colonels.

Our definition is a general one that can be applied to virtually **all jobs**. Clearly, in addition to this general definition, each person has their personal definition and that can change during the course of their life. For example, a minority of long time employees coast toward retirement. In many cases, at this point in their lives, they might define success as getting a good early retirement package. (In one company, this group was identified in their personnel records as R.O.T.J.W.T.U.—which means retired on the job without telling us.)

WHAT DOES IT TAKE TO BE SUCCESSFUL?

Successful people have a better batting average in making choices. Every day, you make choices. You make small, medium and big ones. You make choices about simple matters and complex ones. Some were made in fractions of a second while others took weeks or months. Professionally and personally, you make an incredible number of choices. Although this book focuses on what happens professionally, the basic ideas have broad application in terms of personal decisions. *The choices you make can enhance or detract from your ability to achieve results, develop a favorable reputation and build productive working relationships.*

Every time you communicate you make a choice about the best way to compose your message. Every time you disagree with someone you make a choice about how to resolve the conflict in the best way possible. Every time you set a priority you are making a choice. Perhaps you're faced with a complex problem. But as you reflect on it, you decide it isn't essential to arrive at a decision immediately. It's better to wait. In other cases, you decide to take prompt action. The wide array of the different kinds of choices can be viewed as answers to different questions like who, when, what and how. If you're a manager, you must make innumerable decisions about motivating people, how to coach them, who to hire, who to promote, and so on. You also have to get the cooperation of people who do not work for you.

What do we call someone who makes good choices?

You guessed it. **We say they have better than average common sense.**

I prefer the term common sense; some people prefer to call it good judgment. In this book, *the terms judgment and common sense are used interchangeably* because we frequently use either term to describe people we know who make good choices. The key chapters in this book are devoted to an in-depth analysis of how individuals who have better than average common sense are different, what sets them apart. What is different about them?

1) They have four problem-solving talents.
2) They have three interpersonal competencies.
3) They have a unique set of attributes and attitudes.

The Four Talents
The Common Sense Problem-Solving Model

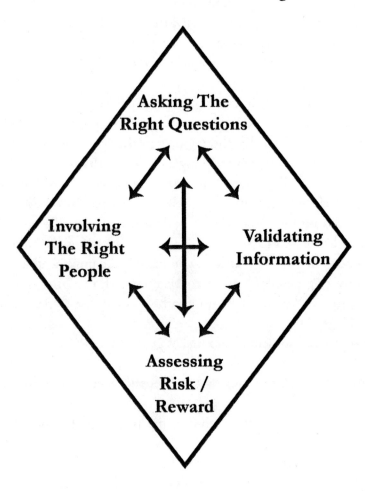

For common sense to be understood, it must be defined in several ways. One definition is **the ability to size up a situation and respond appropriately**. An appropriate response has a positive impact on one or all of the three R's. Every situation is unique. In some situations, only one of these talents is required, but, in most situations, one or more of them come into play.

This process can be an internal monologue. You are in a meeting at work and you disagree with someone. In a matter of seconds, you ask yourself a series of questions like:

> Should I speak up or shut up? If I decide to speak up, what is the best way to serve up my message? What have I got to win or lose? Is the information I have rock solid?

The process can also be interactive. Suppose you are part of team which has been assigned the task of launching a new product. Several people need to be involved. In a one hour meeting with one person or several people you hop scotch all over the place. In one part of this meeting, you can be trying to figure if there are risks you haven't discovered, if you have been accurate in estimating the magnitude of the risk or opportunity. At another time, in the same meeting, you can be attempting to validate a piece of data. At another time, you are looking for questions which you have not asked. You are multitasking—carrying out several processes concurrently.

It should be pointed out that four processes or talents are not mutually exclusive (i.e., you can involve the right person, asking them a question which focuses on risk, and, at the same time, you might be trying to validate some information you have).

One final observation. You can learn how to ask better questions, involve the right people and increase your skills in validating. So, there are many ways you can improve. On the other hand, it can be very difficult for some individuals to modify their approach to risk-taking.

The Three Critical Interpersonal Competencies

It has been frequently pointed out that to do well in sports one must master the basics. The same can be said about any other profession and it is also true of people who have well-honed interpersonal skills. Based on my experience, there are three very fundamental and basic interpersonal competencies: 1) the ability to build productive working relationships based on mutual trust, 2) the ability to influence others based on an other-oriented approach and 3) the ability to use feedback to make course corrections.

It is important to recognize that many of the talents, competencies, attributes and attitudes exhibited by individuals with common sense have *no correlation with intelligence*. Very often when I have asked people to tell me why they are successful, they reply: **"It's Not Rocket Science"**. The clear implication is they do not necessarily regard themselves as being in that group that has genius level IQs.

Franklin Roosevelt, who established an enviable track record of making good choices when facing highly complex issues, had this to say about himself: "I'm not the smartest fellow in the world, but I can sure pick smart colleagues. Because, I am not so smart, I have to surround myself with real talent." Oliver Wendell Holmes Jr., a famous Supreme Court Justice, concurred in that judgment. After meeting Franklin Roosevelt, his comment was: "A second class intellect—but a first rate temperament."

Attributes and Attitudes

It is impossible to achieve the kind of results, reputation and relationship you aspire to without having a high level of ego-strength. This is a term which encompasses a cluster of traits like having a strong work ethic, being free from the need to conform, knowing how to get strokes and using psychological crutches. It is also necessary to have the right attitudes, like being skeptical, knowing there is more than one way to skin a cat, and believing that doing the right thing is the best course to take over the long haul. These attributes and attitudes will be discussed in greater detail near the end of the book.

THE LONG JOURNEY

As a psychologist, I frequently was asked by various companies to help them improve the yardsticks they used in evaluating candidates for promotion. Caterpillar wanted to do a better job of selecting middle level managers in their plants. Banker's Trust wanted better yardsticks to use in selecting branch managers. Merck was expanding overseas and had identified country managers as being key to their success. Johnson & Johnson asked me to examine the job of the first line sales supervisor.

In each of these research projects, I asked management to give me a list of the most successful individuals in these different jobs. I collected as much information as I could about them and interviewed each of them. I ended up being more confused than I was when I started the projects. Some of the best people were well organized, yet some were not. Some were rather autocratic and some were not. Some were very outgoing and others were the strong silent type. Some were quite bright and others were of average intelligence. In short, their differences obscured their commonalities. I remained confused for several years.

The breakthrough came when I asked myself this simple question: **"What do people do everyday in their jobs?"** The answer—they make choices (judgments). That insight led me to focus on the attributes and defining characteristics of individuals who were better at making choices...individuals with above average common sense. This was an exciting breakthrough. This epiphany reminded me of quote by the inventor of the Polaroid camera, Dr. Land, who said: *"Insight is the sudden cessation of stupidity."*

THE CLINCHER

In my fifty years of consulting, I had the opportunity to work with four first-class organizations: Caterpillar, Johnson & Johnson, Merck & Co., and Olin Brass.

After I concluded that common sense was the #1 critical success factor, I remembered a quotation from General Johnson. (Johnson & Johnson, was run for many years by General Robert Wood Johnson. He was, in my view, a management genius. I served as an advisor to several senior executives of the company during the years when sales grew from $1 billion to over $45 billion—a record which was, in part, due to policies and practices put into effect by the General who died in 1968.)

The General wrote a corporate responsibility statement in 1935 which he continuously revised. Below, is one of the versions.

We believe that our first responsibility is to our customers.

Our second responsibility is to those who work with us.

Our third responsibility is to our management.

Our fourth and last responsibility is to our stockholders.

Each of these responsibilities had bullet points under them. Under the third responsibility, the General indicated that managers—

"must be persons of talent, education, experience and ability. They must be persons of *common sense* and full understanding."

THE HUMOR SECTION

At the end of the book, there is a Humor Section. Life is filled with speed bumps. When you hit one, you can cry, get mad, go shopping, go for a run or use humor to maintain your equanimity. In fact, throughout the book, the goal has been to inform and entertain, to combine wisdom and wit.

One of the most famous psychologists of the twentieth century, Abraham Maslow, did a breakthrough study on emotionally healthy individuals. As far as I know, it was the first study of this type. Prior to Maslow, much of the literature about human behavior was authored by professionals who spent their lives (like Freud) working with the mentally ill.

One of Maslow's findings was that healthier people had a philosophical sense of humor. This section has four satirical essays, which are dedicated to Maslow.

◆   ◆   ◆

Author's note: You will find no summary at the conclusion of this book. I have always felt that a summary should be at the beginning of a book instead of at the end. Besides, if I have failed to communicate my ideas in each chapter, a summary can't possibly compensate for this.

Section 1

The Four Problem-Solving Talents

1. Asking the Right Questions
2. Involving the Right People
3. Validating
4. Assessing Risk/Reward

Asking the Right Questions

o o o o o o o o o o o o o o o o o o o o o o o o o o o o o o o o o

"A problem well-stated is half-solved."

—*John Dewey*

Judgment is the process of making choices. All choices are answers to one or more questions. Asking the right questions doesn't guarantee getting the right answer, but it is almost impossible to get the right answer if you are asking the wrong question.

Individuals with good judgment are better at asking questions...questions they ask themselves privately or questions they pose to others They customize their questions to fit the situation. As a result, they make better choices.

CUSTOMIZING QUESTIONS TO FIT THE SITUATION

The most proficient business leaders develop an arsenal of questioning techniques. They realize that different situations require different types of questions an important insight which seems to elude many people. They wear different "questioning hats," depending on the situation. These are the hats of:

- The Archer

- The Fisherman

- The Communicator

- The Gray Fox

3

- The Talmudic Scholar

- The Skeptic

THE ARCHER: HITTING THE BULL'S-EYE

When the archer pulls back his bowstring and lets the arrow fly straight toward the center of the target, he's doing the same thing the superior questioner does. He takes aim and gets right to the heart of the matter. Hitting the bull's-eye involves determining the best question that immediately gets to the root of the problem and crystallizes the pivotal issue. Once the true issue is exposed, the problem can be solved quickly and efficiently. When you're at the beginning of a problem solving process, finding the question that hits the bull's-eye takes you a quantum leap forward. Often the bull's-eye question is what I call "decision determining." It's the question that, by itself, points the way to the best decision.

Once, my daughter, Jenna, sent me a wonderful birthday card. On the front of the card, it said:

"Every time I have a problem I ask myself what would my father do?"

Inside the card, it said:

"Then I ask the question: How can I get him to do it?"

Besides illustrating how one question can crystallize critical issues, this anecdote also illustrates a strategy people successfully employ: putting yourself in the shoes of someone you admire and then asking how he or she would proceed under similar circumstances. It also highlights the fundamental fact that we don't have to be totally self-reliant. In fact, more often than not, when we initially explore an issue, the first question should be: Who can help me?

Unfortunately, the problems that confront most of us are usually more complex than the ones facing my daughter. In the majority of cases, many variables have to be considered. For example, if you are an auto manufacturer, one of your top priorities has to be cost, because in certain segments of the market you'll need to price the car competitively and still make a profit. The question you ask is: "How can we manufacture this car at the least possible cost?" This question leads to a cascade of related questions, like: "How can we design a car that's easy to assemble in order to cut labor costs?" "How can we cut costs without decreasing quality? In the end, you can find yourself struggling with a staggering surplus of legitimate objectives to achieve. Faced with such complexity, it's easy to get lost and lose sight of the overriding goal you're trying to achieve. That's when hitting the bull's-eye can be of enormous value.

Donald Petersen, then president of Ford, hit the bull's-eye in a discussion with his top designers, as told in Managing on the Edge, by Richard Tanner Pascale.

> "Petersen had come to the design center to review proposals for a new Thunderbird. Once a breath of fresh air in Ford's line, the Thunderbird had become about as exciting as a cement truck. "He was shown the customer sketches of the big boring boxes," said one source. "Ford designers, truth be told, hated their own designs. They had come to the unhappy state through attrition; year after year they had championed daring ideas and been shot down by top management. There was only one kind of car headquarters wanted: A Car Just Like Last Year's."
>
> After reviewing several prototypes, Petersen probed: "Is this the car you would like to drive?" There was a long silence. Generally, people at Ford had learned not to say what they thought. "Absolutely not. I wouldn't want that car parked in my driveway," Ford's Chief Design Executive, Jack Telnack, answered frankly. Petersen inquired further. Encouraged, the designers rolled out their clay models, their dream designs. Functionality, taking the driver seriously, appealing to the consumer's better judgment rather than to the market research department's lowest common denominator: headquarters was bound to hate it. Instead, Petersen gave the go-ahead to design a radically new car. Emboldened, Design showed him their ideas for a daring midsized car design where Ford sells most of its automobiles. Petersen liked what he saw, eventually investing $3.2 billion in the now famous "jellybean" cars the Taurus and the Sable."

One moral of the story is that when, from time to time, you have conflicting objectives, you need to step back, put things in perspective, and make absolutely sure that the most important goal is not forgotten.

Another moral is that the bull's-eye question changes over time. Many years before Petersen ran Ford Motor Company, it was run by its founder, Henry Ford. In the first part of the twentieth century, the decision determining question for Ford was simply cost. If Ford could not build a car people could afford to buy, the automobile as a product would never get off the ground. So the correct bull's-eye question then was not about balancing cost and quality, it was, "How do we build a car that people can afford to buy?"

It's clear from these examples that many of yesterday's on target questions will not solve today's problems. Frequently I am in situations when I say to myself: "What are the questions I need to be asking myself at this point in time?" I take inspiration from a large poster I have in my office, depicting a gorilla with a perplexed look on his face holding one hand over his forehead. The caption reads: "Just when I knew all of life's answers, they changed the questions."

Warren Buffett, the legendary investment wizard, is now one of the richest men in the world. One of his talents is the ability to ask decision determining questions which others had not asked.

Buffett was an ardent admirer of Graham, the father of value analysis. Accordingly, he was determined to identify companies whose stock was cheap, relative to its potential value. But he went beyond looking at such conventional measures as price-to-earnings ratio, debt, projected growth in earnings per share, etc. What set Buffett apart? How did he go that extra mile? What additional question did he ask that others hadn't? You may be surprised.

Buffett reasoned that over an extended period of time, it was very likely that any given company would be managed by someone who had reached his or her "level of incompetence." He decided that he should invest in businesses that even a dummy could run because sooner or later a dummy will. "Could a dummy run this business?" was the bull's-eye question that played a major role in helping him to accumulate his untold wealth.

Perhaps your intuition will shape the decision determining question. Alfred Sloan ran General Motors for almost forty years. He had a track record of consistently making great decisions. He said:

"An essential aspect of our management philosophy is the factual approach to business judgment. The final act of business judgment is, of course, intuitive."

Verne Willaman started his career as a sales representative and finished it as a member of the board of directors of Johnson & Johnson. While he was division sales manager, he set numerous performance records, many of which remain unbeaten years later. When asked the reasons for his success, he said he had hired good people. How did he do this? He followed a very specific process. First, he conducted a thorough initial screening. Then he invited the candidate back for a second, longer interview. Then, he put the candidate through more paces, including tests. And finally, he asked himself, "Would I like to go on a cruise with this person for three weeks?" If the answer to this gut level question was no, the person didn't get hired.

Listen to your gut. In many cases, it will—and should—be decision determining.

THE FISHERMAN: CASTING A WIDE NET

If you're going to get a gold medal in the Asking Questions Olympics, you need the ability to zero in on whatever is decision determining. You also need the patience and skill to ask an incredibly large number of questions to make sure you learn enough to make the best decision.

Someone who really knew the power of casting a wide net was Sam Walton. His case provides one of the most dramatic examples of how big the payoff can be when your questions cast a wide net. In his autobiography, *Sam Walton: Made in America—My Story*, there are many illustrations of how he relentlessly and vigorously picked the brains of everyone.

As an example, Don Soderquest, Vice Chairman and CEO of Wal-Mart, tells this story of Walton's visit to a discount store in another market:

> I could hear him asking this clerk, "Well, how frequently do you order? Uhhuh. How much do you order? And if you order on a Tuesday, when does the merchandise come in?" He's writing everything she says down in a little blue spiral notebook. Then Sam gets down on his

hands and knees and he's looking under this stack table, and he opens the sliding doors and says, "How do you know how much you've got under here when you're placing that order?"

A quote from Mr. Sam:

> "I probably visited more headquarters' offices of more discounters than anybody else—ever. I would just show up and say, "Hi, I'm Sam Walton from Bentonville, Arkansas. We've got a few stores out there, and I'd like to visit with Mr. So-and-So—whoever the head of the company was—about his business." And as often as not, they'd let me in, maybe out of curiosity, and I'd ask lots of questions about pricing and distribution, whatever. I learned a lot that way."

Walton was on a learning curve. He wanted to know anything that would be of value to him, so he asked endless questions. Being thoroughly informed has many advantages. One is that it minimizes the chances of unpleasant surprises.

THE COMMUNICATOR: PROBING TO UNDERSTAND

We have all experienced communication problems. We have all been misunderstood from time to time, or we have gravely misunderstood others. My experience has taught me that a fairly high percentage of communication problems can be avoided if individuals did a better job of probing—asking the kinds of questions that lead to full and complete understanding.

The value of probing is illustrated by an amusing anecdote, which was used by Clark Clifford, legal advisor to several U.S. Presidents, when he was teaching a course in contracts at St. Louis University Law School. This anecdote is found in his book, *Counsel to the President*:

> "In this class, I stressed the importance of reaching a complete and full understanding, a "meeting of the minds," between two persons entering into a contract. Often, I said, people thought they had such understanding until they were ready to execute the agreement, at which time

they found out that each had a different notion of what the contract meant. I illustrated my point with a story that has always remained one of my favorites; I think that I eventually told it to every president I ever knew, as well as to most of my friends. It goes as follows:

A man walking down the street noticed a sign in the window of a restaurant that said, SPECIAL TODAY—RABBIT STEW. He said to himself, "That's a favorite of mine," and went in to order the stew. After he had taken three or four bites, which did not taste quite right, he asked the waiter to call over the proprietor. "By any chance is there any horsemeat in this rabbit stew?" the customer asked. "Well, now that you ask, there is some," responded the owner. "What is the proportion?" asked the man. "Fifty-fifty," was the reply. Now, most people would have felt that no further questions were needed, that there was a clear understanding. But this man pursued the issue. "What do you mean by fifty-fifty?" he asked, and the proprietor replied, "One horse to one rabbit."

In this kind of exchange, what happens all too frequently? We end the dialogue prematurely. We stop, thinking we have understood the entire situation, when in reality we haven't.

If you are going to get better in understanding the messages you are receiving, learning to ask probing questions is essential. The next story illustrates how the failure to probe can lead to very undesirable consequences.

A stranger in a small town came across a man walking a dog. The stranger asked the man "Does your dog bite?" The man said, "No." The stranger reached down to pet the dog, which immediately bit him. The stranger angrily pulled away his bleeding hand, and screamed, "You told me your dog didn't bite!" The man replied, "You didn't ask if this was my dog."

Have you ever been bitten because you failed to probe?

THE GRAY FOX: THE DEVIL IS IN THE DETAILS

The Gray Fox is a battle-scarred senior executive. In the past, he may have approved plans to launch a product, buy a company, or build facilities—plans he would not have approved if he had all the facts when the decision was made. Consequently, the facts have come to haunt him. His experiences have reinforced the Gray Fox's natural skepticism. He has become a reality-centered paranoid. He is convinced that the devil is in the details. He asks questions that will help root the devil out before he signs off on the project.

Every top-level executive has been traumatized by situations like this, many of them leading to major losses and some to expensive lawsuits. When clauses in contracts are based on inaccurate cost calculations, for example, the result can be years of litigation and big-time problems with shareholders. The Gray Fox casts a wide net, like the fisherman, but with the express purpose of asking questions that will ferret out any and all potential complications. The fisherman is trying to learn. The Gray Fox is trying to find the time bomb before it goes off.

A few years back, I met with Ron Brenner, one of the top executives in Johnson & Johnson, just after he had made a presentation to Dave Clare, the president, on a proposal to construct a new building in Spring House, Pennsylvania. Ron was happy because the project had been approved, but he was upset about some questions the president, Dave Clare, had asked. One being, "How many seats are there in the auditorium?"

From Ron's point of view, this was a nitpicking, inappropriate, and silly question. It was hard for him to understand that Dave was exploring all the intricacies of the proposal to see if there was a hidden time bomb. Dave's concern was justified and stemmed from the fact that this was Ron's first major undertaking in this area. Dave wanted to satisfy himself that Ron had done all of his homework so he delved into the details.

The Gray Fox exerts every effort to make sure he doesn't end up ducking shrapnel when an overlooked detail explodes down the road.

THE TALMUDIC SCHOLAR: ON THE OTHER HAND

I call this hat the Talmudic Scholar because it reflects one of the hallmarks of Hebrew scholars making every effort to see both sides of any issue. This is the hat you wear to put things in balance, in proper perspective, by viewing things from at least two points of view. When balance and perspective are key, the superior questioner asks questions that will reveal both sides of the issue.

At a dinner party, the British playwright George Bernard Shaw found himself seated next to the most beautiful actress in England. Stunning as she was, however, she was also a bit of a dimwit. Rambling on during the meal, she turned to Shaw and asked "Wouldn't it be wonderful if we had a baby? It would be the most beautiful and brightest child in the world!" To which Shaw replied, "Perhaps, madam, but what if it had my looks and your brains?"

Many people envy me because I travel extensively in my work. "How wonderful it must be to get to visit all sorts of different places," they gush, "eat in wonderful restaurants and stay in first class hotels." They're just thinking about the positives while they totally ignore the negatives. People who jump to the conclusion that travel is always an exhilarating experience have a distorted view. On the one hand, travel is great, on the other hand, travel can be a pain in the neck—being away from the family, standing in endless lines for security checks, and waiting four or five hours because of flight delays or cancellations.

Similarly, I have found that people who are trained in disciplines requiring great precision (such as finance and engineering, for example) frequently and predictably develop a distorted point of view and make bad decisions because of an overemphasis on what is more objective, factual, and quantifiable. In many situations, they do not take into account the most important variables, which are subjective, not factual and qualitative.

The following example from Harvey MacKay's *Swim With the Sharks* shows just how wrong we can be if we don't recognize the importance of intangibles when drawing conclusions.

"There's a story going the rounds that a manager who couldn't use his concert tickets for Schubert's *Unfinished Symphony* gave them to his work-study management executive—in nonjargon, the efficiency expert—and received the following report after the performance:

For considerable periods, the four oboe players had nothing to do. Their number should be reduced, and their work spread over the whole orchestra.

Forty violins were playing identical notes. This seems unnecessary duplication, and this section should be drastically cut. If a larger volume of sound is required, this could be achieved through an electronic amplifier.

Much effort was absorbed in the playing of demi/semiquavers. This seems an excessive refinement, and it is recommended that all notes be rounded to the nearest semiquaver. If this were done, it should be possible to use trainees and lower-grade operators.

No useful purpose is served by repeating with horns the passage that has already been handled by the strings. If all such redundant passes were eliminated, the concert could be reduced to twenty minutes. If Schubert had attended to these matters, he probably would have been able to finish his symphony after all."

THE SKEPTIC: QUESTIONING THE CONVENTIONAL WISDOM

To repeat, the individuals who have the greatest chance of achieving their goals are better at making choices. Choices, when you put them under a microscope, are really answers to questions. And those who develop the skill of decision-making are, to start with, skeptical. They don't take things at face value; they don't assume that conventional wisdom is correct. They don't accept traditional organizational practices without questioning them.

Take the case of Galen (the fountainhead of traditional wisdom at the time) and Harvey (the skeptic).

Galen was what you might call a world-class MD. His contributions to medicine were many and varied, and his practice really took off when he moved to Rome in AD 161. One of his claims to fame was that he ran an "HMO" that catered to Roman emperors. Since he always had to be available when these powerful people needed him, he had copious free time, so he wrote a textbook on anatomy. The book became the bible of anatomy and was used for hundreds of years. In this book, he asserted that blood moved to and fro in the blood vessels until it was finally consumed. This became the conventional wisdom.

Then in the first half of the seventeenth century, along came a skeptical Englishman, Sir William Harvey, who earned his place in the history of medicine (and a knighthood) by discovering that blood actually circulated through the body.

In his studies of the heart, Harvey observed the valves in the major arteries leading to and away from the organ's four chambers. No one else had ever thought to question Galen's theory about blood circulation and no one had therefore ever wondered about the valves. Harvey, however, was a skeptic. Not worrying about the conventional wisdom, he asked an obvious but until then overlooked question: What are those valves for?

Questioning the purpose of the valves led Harvey to the conclusion that blood circulates through the body and the heart acts as the pump. In asking this question, Harvey upset assumptions that had endured for almost 1,500 years. Over this period of time, a large number of people studied medicine, many very smart people, but obviously not enough skeptics.

People with good judgment are like good scientists. They question. They look for proof. So if you make up your mind to ask more questions and make fewer assumptions, you too, like Harvey, might be knighted someday!

ASKING THE WRONG QUESTIONS

Essentially, in the question-asking process, there are two things that can go wrong. First, as we see in the case of all those people who thought about blood circulation over a period of 1,500 years, no one was asking questions about the purpose of valves in the heart. This was an error of omission.

The second way things go amiss is when the wrong questions are asked. The wrong questions are not on target. They are imprecise or not sufficiently complete. When you ask the wrong question, it's like getting on the wrong train that will not take you to your desired destination.

As we will see from the following examples, when we ask the wrong question it may preclude us from identifying the right question. We can become myopic or develop tunnel vision.

I am a tennis player. When you play tennis on a hot day, your hands become sweaty. You can then have trouble hitting shots because your grip becomes less firm and the racket handle turns when you hit the ball. I found this to be a real problem with my game, so I asked myself: "How can I prevent moisture from collecting on my hand?"

Each time I was in a pro shop, I tried to find solutions to my problem. I bought wristbands to prevent the sweat from running down my arm. I bought sprays that were supposed to absorb the moisture. I bought shorts that had a piece of toweling sewn onto the outside of the pockets, enabling me to frequently wipe my hands. When I saw Bjorn Borg on TV take saw-dust out of his pocket and use it to absorb moisture, I rushed out to the lumberyard and acquired some sawdust. All my efforts were in vain. Nothing I tried worked.

I experimented with different solutions for seventeen years.

Then, one day my friend, Eric, arrived for a match carrying three rackets. I assumed he was following a practice used by the pros carrying several rackets in order to have a spare when the strings break. Really good players hit the ball so hard that they often break racket strings in the middle of matches. People who play at my level hardly ever break strings.

I immediately teased Joe about this crude and obvious display of attempted one-upmanship trying to intimidate me by bringing several rackets. To my surprise, my friend replied that was not what he had in mind at all. He was not trying to put me at a psychological disadvantage. He said that whenever the handle of his racket became damp, he exchanged it for a fresh racket.

My seventeen-year-old problem was solved in a flash.

Where did I go wrong? I had asked a good question! "How can I prevent moisture from collecting on my hand?" is a logical question. Because it was a legitimate and plausible question, I thought I was on the right train.

In this case, my question only addressed part of the problem. If I had asked myself, "What can I do to have a dry racket and a dry hand?" I would have gotten on the right train. Having asked a question dealing with only part of the total problem, I was inevitably and permanently doomed to failure.

Once you get on the train to nowhere, you can stay on it for days, weeks, months, or in my case, seventeen years. Was my experience one-of-a-kind? Am I the only person who wasted time and effort pursuing the wrong questions? I think not.

Here is a story told by Joel Barker in his book, *Future Edge*.

"As anyone who has followed the compact disc technology knows, Sony was one of the first into the fray. Their first portable CD player was hailed for its technological prowess. One hi-fi magazine called it "second generation technology the first time around."

Why was Sony the leader? The obvious answer comes from examining when they started their research of laser music discs: the early 1970s.

It sounds great until you also learn that around 1976 they stopped their research, concluding that laser discs were not appropriate for music. Curious, don't you think?

It wasn't until 1979 that they were induced back into the audio laser disc business by Phillips of the Netherlands. Phillips called Sony to talk about establishing a world standard for audio CDs, because it knew that Sony had done extensive work in the area.

Typical of the Japanese, Sony didn't say, "That's a stupid idea because we've already checked it out." Instead, they invited Phillips to come to Japan and talk about it.

Phillips sent a small team. Again, typical of the Japanese, Sony assembled the team who had done the research. And, again typically, they let the Phillips people make their presentation first.

As the story goes, the Phillips research started with a disclaimer stating that they knew Sony was way ahead of them, so whatever Sony wanted to do was fine. Then they proceeded to show them the prototype of the laser music disc they were working on about one-half inch larger in diameter than today's disc.

"We think this is about the right size," they said.

Now, I can't be positive what the Japanese thought as they saw that little disc, but I'm willing to speculate. I'll bet it was the Japanese equivalent of "Oh, s___!"

Because, guess what size disc the Japanese had been working on the entire time? Remember the old paradigm LPs twelve inches in diameter! That was their model. And if a disc one third that size could hold more than an hour's worth of music, what do you think a twelve-inch disc could hold? About eighteen hours of music!

And the Japanese looked at that eighteen hours of capacity and asked themselves two very intelligent questions. How would we program the eighteen hours? One hour of Sinatra plus one hour of Beethoven plus one hour of the Beatles plus...well, you get the idea. The second was: How do you price it $199.95?

Those are both important questions, if you have accepted the size as a certainty. And they had."

The Sony managers were in a mental rut. They had tunnel vision. When this happens, you fail to ask the appropriate question, but with 20/20 hindsight the question and the answer are obvious.

The Vietnam War was one of the most dramatic examples in this century of a group of people who got on the wrong train. In his book, *In Retrospect*, Robert McNamara, Secretary of Defense to John F. Kennedy and Lyndon Johnson, details the mistakes and misjudgments that led to the disastrous involvement of the United States in the Vietnam War. McNamara writes:

"We [the members of President Kennedy's cabinet] failed to ask the five most basic questions: Was it true that the fall of South Vietnam would trigger the fall of all Southeast Asia? Would that constitute a grave threat to the West's security? What kind of conventional or guerrilla war might develop? Could we win it with U.S. troops fighting alongside the South Vietnamese? Should we not know the answer to all these questions before deciding whether to commit troops?"

Sobering evidence for how essential it is to ask the right questions? I think so.

POINTS TO REMEMBER

Judgment is the process of making choices. All choices are answers to some question. Good judgment is partly based on knowing how to tailor the question or questions to the situation. You need be able to wear the hats of:

- The Archer

- The Fisherman

- The Communicator

- The Gray Fox

- The Talmudic Scholar

- The Skeptic

In some instances, you will be like an archer who wants to hit the center of the target with the decision-determining question. In others, you will need to be like a fisherman with a net; you'll need to ask many people many questions. To develop full understanding, you need to probe. At other times, you'll need to be sure, like a Talmudic scholar, that your perspective is complete such that you see the issues from the "on-the-other-hand" angle. There can be great rewards in being skeptical and questioning conventional wisdom. If making presentations to upper management is part of your job, you need to anticipate all the questions that you might be asked.

Finally, you don't have to be smart enough to ask all the relevant questions. You have to be smart enough to get the right answer to one question: "Who can help me?"

Involving the Right People

◆

(Leverage)

Suppose two people were equal in all respects but one. Suppose Person A thought they knew all the answers. Person B believed in the motto of President Woodrow Wilson, who said, *"I need all the brains I have and all I can borrow."* Who will be more successful in making better choices in their personal and professional lives?

As we discussed in the last chapter, the ability to ask questions that are situation appropriate is one of the common denominators of winners. Regardless of the situation, one of the questions that is imbedded in their minds is "Who should I involve?"

We involve others for several different reasons, depending on the situation. These reasons are:

- Saving Time

- Capitalizing on the Expert's Expertise

- Two Heads Are Better than One

- Breaking a Mental Roadblock

- Validating: The Sanity Check

The second part of this chapter deals with the state of affairs that exists when you are not the final decision maker and when involving others is not an option. But first, let us consider what happens when you are the final decision maker. When you make the final decision, *you can make quicker, better decisions with less stress by involving the right people.*

This is one of the most important of all talents and one of the rarest. For example, I met one man in 1965 that had this ability and it was twenty-two years later before I met anyone in his class. The name of the second man is Bill Weldon, who became the CEO of Johnson& Johnson.

SAVING TIME

Let me use buying a car as an example. Buying a car shopping around and playing cat-and-mouse games with salesmen is in the top five on my list of things-I-don't-like-doing.

I went through the list of all of my friends, looking for someone who enjoyed buying cars; a person who was not only very knowledgeable about cars in general, but who also liked to shop around and knew where to get the best price. I found such a person and consulted with him. He gave me some quick, coherent advice based on his extensive research and experience. I bought a great car about a week later and paid what I considered a very good price. No stress (well, almost no stress), no long hours of shopping around, reading car magazines, taking endless test-drives. Instead, I was free to devote that time to making the best use of my talents.

Imagine repeating the strategy I used with the car with equally positive results in twenty or thirty other situations in the course of a year. Think not only of the value of making a better decision than you probably would have made on your own, but think of the time you could save. Now think of how you could use that time focusing on issues that make the best use of your talents. It's like going through life hitting doubles instead of singles.

CAPITALIZING ON THE EXPERT'S EXPERTISE

A classic story that comes to mind is the tale of New York City and the Central Park ice-skating rink. Over several years, the city had spent millions trying to get a rink in the park to function effectively. No matter what the city tried, nothing worked. A bit desperate, the mayor asked a young contractor, Donald Trump, to tackle the problem.

Trump immediately asked himself the pivotal question: "Who are the experts in building and maintaining ice-skating rinks?" To him, the answer was obvious…the Canadians. Trump called the head of the Canadian Ice Hockey Association, and solved the problem in record time. Recognizing the value of going straight to the experts, instead of fooling around in an area he knew nothing about, Trump saved New York a lot of money.

Ann Landers, the famous advice giver, got the job of writing a column because she was so discerning in knowing exactly who could help her with different types of problems. When the Chicago Sun Times screened 30 applicants for this job, each was given the same three problems to solve; the types of actual problems submitted by readers. Ann Landers quickly contacted the three different experts who could help her the most. Her ability to tap into the right experts got her the job!

When he was elected president, Kennedy grappled with the Vietnam problem, soliciting the opinions of many people. The key question he should have asked himself was, "Who has had the most experience with Vietnam?" (In almost all situations, it is a good practice to ask yourself, "Who has had a problem similar to the one I have?"

The answer: General Charles deGaulle. DeGaulle, with his military background and intimate familiarity with the Vietnamese (Vietnam was a French colony from 1883 until 1945) was a perfect paradigm of the best kind of source: a person with great knowledge and experience but with no ulterior motive. When Kennedy and deGaulle finally met, the General advised the President that it was impossible to win a war in Vietnam and that the real task was to find a face-saving way to disengage. In the 20/20 hindsight of history, his advice seems heartbreakingly on target.

Two Heads Are Better than One

In addition to picking the brains of people who have an expertise we do not have, we must also recognize that when we try to solve a problem on our own, we are limited by our own experience or point of view or we cannot see the forest for the trees. Two heads are better than one is a well-known saying; of course, it could be three or four or even a dozen heads.

Surely you have had the experience of failing to solve a problem by working on your own. Someone else comes along, and the two of you kick the problem around, coming up with alternatives and building on each other's ideas. Pow! Much to your delight, you identify a good solution. And there is no doubt that neither you nor the other person could ever have found the answer working independently.

As you kick ideas around with someone, many good things can happen. You discover an alternative answer to a problem that was not on your radar screen. You find a quicker or easier way to execute a plan. You discover some highly relevant information that you did not have before.

We are all familiar with many well-known examples of how two heads are better than one. We are living in the middle of two technology explosions. One is the biotechnology revolution, which could never have happened without the pioneering DNA work of Watson and Crick. It is doubtful whether they could have solved this puzzle by working independently. With respect to the information technology revolution, it is doubtful that Jobs or Wozanky, working alone, could have put the Apple Computer company on the map or that Bill Gates would have been able to make Microsoft into a powerhouse without the help of Paul Allen.

Walt Disney drew a cartoon of a mouse. He thought he would call the mouse Mortimer. His wife suggested the name Mickey. I am glad he talked to his wife, because it is hard for me to imagine that a cartoon character called Mortimer Mouse would have achieved worldwide fame.

BREAKING A MENTAL ROADBLOCK

Sometimes, the help of others takes on more subtle forms. When my son was ten years old, he asked me to help him with a math assignment, which involved things called "*unions*" and "*sets*". As these terms had no meaning for me, I asked him to explain them. When he was finished with his explanation, he suddenly understood the assignment. He looked up at me with total astonishment and said, "You just helped me and you don't even understand the problem!"

This happens all the time. You have a problem. You haven't found a good solution, and you're getting frustrated. By trying to explain your dilemma to a third party, you discover the solution. Has this happened to you? Absolutely. Does it happen as frequently as it should? I doubt it.

VALIDATING "THE SANITY CHECK"

Involving others can provide a great way to confirm your ideas, test your objectivity, and provide a sanity check.

For example, during the Korean conflict, President Truman was ready to fire General Douglas MacArthur for insubordination. He was ninety-nine percent sure of his decision, but wanted another opinion before making a final determination, so he gave his files on MacArthur to General George Marshall. Marshall agreed with Truman's assessment of the situation, and Truman proceeded with far greater comfort than if he had not asked for help.

Time and time again, I find that people who move to high levels in organizations have more than their fair share of common sense. People who have common sense go out of their way to double-check, verify, or otherwise validate their opinions.

On the surface, the different reasons for involving others listed above seem to be similar, but, actually, there are significant differences. When I pick the brain of an expert, they have much more experience and knowledge than I have. This is not the same as two heads are better than one, which is when your skills, database, and/or point of view are different from mine. Breaking a mental roadblock has two players: One who is confused and one who facilitates self-realization on the part of the first player by asking some clarifying questions. The dynamic of the sanity check is "I think I am right, but I want to be sure."

◆   ◆   ◆

When we consider situations in which you are not the final decision maker, the reasons for involving people, which we have outlined above, still apply; however, two more must be added.

GETTING BUY-IN

In your work, there are many times you don't have the final authority and your success often depends on getting "buy- in." You can't make progress without getting the endorsement, agreement, or cooperation of various stakeholders. There are many examples that prove that this idea is not well understood. I think of a recent but typical example of a marketing group that prepared some material that was going to be used by sales representatives. No one thought to get input from managers in the sales organization! Not surprisingly, when the sales folks got involved they found all kinds of major issues that had not been addressed.

When you solicit the views of various stakeholders, you focus on two goals: (1) you want the final result to be better and (2) you want to get support for your project.

PERFECTING THE MESSAGE: THE DRESS REHEARSAL

Suppose you have an important presentation to make to upper management and you decide to run the presentation by four or five people (separately) before you make your final preparation. If this is done properly

- You become more comfortable and confident that you can answer any questions.

- You discover possible objections that you may have to address.

- You find out how to fine-tune your message so you will not be misunderstood.

I once had an appointment with the president of a company in Stamford, Connecticut, to discuss a consulting project. When I arrived, he asked me to sit down, and then started talking about a completely different subject. I knew nothing about this subject, and I wasn't at all sure why he was trying to discuss it with me. But I kept my mouth shut, and I'm glad I did. After about an hour, he suddenly got up from the chair where he was sitting, walked over to his phone, called the chairman of the board, and sold him on the idea he had just reviewed with me. I was the audience for the president's dress rehearsal.

I once worked with an extraordinarily talented real estate developer, Eric Eichler. When I was with him, he would usually have to interrupt our conversation to take important calls. When his secretary told him who was on the line, Eric would tell her to hold for a minute. I watched as he obviously went through a mental dress rehearsal. Several questions flashed through his mind. What was the person likely to say? How was he going to respond? What points did he want to make?

What happens during a dress rehearsal? As you convey your idea to another person, you pick up clues about how your message is being received. It's almost as if you're viewing a person's brain waves through a glass window in the forehead; you can tell by eye movement, facial expression, body language, and actual spoken questions and responses how your message is working or where it is falling apart. You can refine your spiel and recognize the holes in your thinking before putting yourself on the line.

There is absolutely no question that informal dress rehearsals can dramatically improve your success rate in making presentations to management. When the lack of a dress rehearsal results in the failure to sell a good idea, the excuse people use is that they didn't have the time. Guess what? The reason they didn't have the time is that they are inept at leveraging.

INVOLVING OTHERS AND THE OPEN MIND

So far, we have discussed the different ways to involve people, depending on the situation. However, the best people are continually learning from others. There are groups of people who think they have all the answers and it is not necessary to involve others.

In his book *Paterno: By The Book* Joe Paterno, the famous Penn State football coach, said, "In my third or fourth year as a head coach something like 20 years after I started coaching I also finally learned to appreciate picking up an idea from somebody else, anybody else. Until then, I was too sure of myself to listen to others, and I hurt myself as a result."

In my experience, Paterno's first 20 years were more the rule than the exception. He was older than 40 before he figured out that while the Lone Ranger might be a hero in Hollywood; lone rangers are seldom the winners in the real world.

A person with the opposite attitude was the famous American author, poet, and philosopher Ralph Waldo Emerson who said: "Every person I meet is in some way my superior and I can find a way to learn from them."

As an interesting case in point, I am convinced that one of the reasons General Johnson became so successful was he exemplified Emerson's dictum. The General lived for some time in Princeton, New Jersey. He would invite a diverse group of people—academics from Princeton University, professional people, and businessmen—and he would pick their brains. If he found he learned nothing from a person, they were never invited back.

During a lecture, I had told a group that you never know when or how you are going to meet someone who could help you. I pointed out that business people like themselves are constantly sitting together on planes with strangers. Instead of lying to each other about how important they are (which is what usually happens), I suggested it would be smarter to find out what they could learn.

One participant took my advice to heart as he boarded his flight back to Memphis. Sitting next to him just happened to be a woman from IBM who was one of the most organized people he had ever met. Since this man had world-class problems with time management and organization, for the next two hours, he picked this woman's brain on the subject. On that short trip from New York to Memphis, he learned more about how to get organized than he had learned in his whole life before meeting her.

If you want a major competitive advantage and you want to increase the chances of attaining your personal goals, you must learn how to be a talent scout.

As I get to know people, I keep asking myself, "What is their knowledge or experience base? What particular talents do they have? Do they complement me in some way? What can I learn from them?"

Sometimes knowing who can help you is self-evident. Sometimes it's not. Once you know your purpose for enlisting help, it may be only a short step to determining who you're going to contact. If you require functional expertise, the choice may be obvious. However, you may need a deeper level of knowledge about possible sources of help. For instance, if you need help coming up with a creative idea, you want to talk to the person in your organization who is most likely to have a truly original thought. If you want a critique of a presentation, you probably go to a different person. For advice on how to influence top management, you may need to seek out someone else.

LEVERAGE: THE EPITOME OF INVOLVING OTHERS

What does leverage mean to you?

When you pose that question to a group of scientists, they immediately come up with examples from physics. In physics class, you learned that by using the right set of pulleys one person alone could lift something weighing over 5,000 pounds. In other words, by using leverage, a person is capable of accomplishing feats he could never accomplish without it. Archimedes, the Greek mathematician and inventor, was positive he could move the Earth if he had the right fulcrum.

The same principle applies to decision-making. Interpersonal leverage is the process of capitalizing on the talents of others.

If you ask finance people about their interpretation of leverage, they use an example involving different outcomes relative to buying stock.

Suppose you decided to buy $100,000 of General Electric stock and you sold it after it tripled. You would have a pretax profit of $200,000. However, if you had leveraged your investment by going on margin, you would have purchased the shares by putting $10,000 down and obtaining a loan from the broker for $90,000. If you sold the stock for $300,000 and paid off the loan of $90,000, you would be $210,000 ahead. Instead of multiplying your money by a factor of 3, you would have multiplied it by a factor of 21 (minus whatever interest had to be paid on the loan). However, in the case of interpersonal leverage, you are borrowing brains rather than money: There are no interest charges and no taxes.

The ability to involve the right people is one of the most necessary and one of the rarest competencies, and the payoffs can be enormous. Thomas Edison, probably one of the greatest inventors in history, is a prime example. Thomas Edison once said, "I'm a good sponge. I absorb ideas and put them to use. Most of the ideas first belonged to people who didn't bother to develop them."

Hypothetically, if Edison had lived on a desert island with no human contact but all kinds of equipment, in his lifetime, he might have gotten 50 patents approved. He actually had 1,093 approved because of his ability to leverage his talents.

HOW LEVERAGE CAN BACKFIRE

In the examples of buying a car, the skating rink, and the advice column, success does not hinge merely on asking someone else for help. It hinges on asking the right person(s). When you set out to capitalize on the talents of others, it is critical to ensure that their talents are the right ones for the job. It is critical to take the good advice and leave behind the bad. When you pick the wrong people, leveraging works against you instead of for you. It is a double-edged sword, as in the example of financial leverage when you buy a stock, if the stock goes down rather than up you can sustain big losses.

The Clinton administration's healthcare reform project—an example of the negative consequences of involving the wrong people—was a dismal and total failure. I'm not the only one who thinks so. I'm sure that if you were to assemble twelve leading experts on health care, assuming they were politically neutral, they would agree that the plan put forward by the administration was fundamentally flawed and would have created problems more serious than the ones it would have solved. Both Republicans and Democrats generally agree that the whole affair was botched. In various interviews, President Clinton has been very open about his disappointment in the way in which it was handled.

To spearhead the healthcare reform effort, Clinton chose his wife, Hillary Rodham Clinton, and a consultant, Ira Magaziner. Both are smart, motivated people, but wrong for the job.

Being the wrong people, the First Lady and Magaziner not surprisingly latched on to the wrong process. They involved 500 health experts, who formed 34 committees, which identified 840 decisions to be made. If a camel is a horse designed by a committee, then the healthcare plan was destined to be the mother of all camels. With the wrong people at the helm, to mix metaphors, healthcare reform was like a ship that went off course as soon as it left the dock.

Because of the political split in Congress, Clinton couldn't get enough votes for the plan unless he won over every potential ally. But because he had picked the wrong advisors, potential friends were pushed into neutral or enemy camps. Instead of getting buy-in from critical people, the healthcare captains alienated them. Enemies were created when allies were needed. After more than two years of work, no healthcare plan was passed.

Clinton's failure to consult the appropriate people had ramifications far beyond health care reform. As one reporter put it, "It was the most serious political defeat of his presidency, and contributed no doubt to the Republicans' victory in the congressional elections that year."

What Clinton needed was not intellectual talent, but political talent people who knew what sort of plan would pass through Congress. Clinton should have first involved people who had in-depth knowledge and experience about the ways of Washington, people like George Mitchell, Lloyd Bentsen, Leon Panetta, and Daniel Moynihan, to name a few. There are few guarantees in life, but if Clinton had involved the right people, his chances of achieving health care reform would have been much higher.

POINTS TO REMEMBER

A good point to keep in mind is that attitudes are self-reinforcing.

A Core Attitude: Leverage

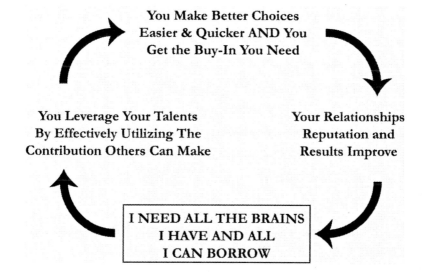

It's not enough just to know you need help. You have to be discerning in identifying who can help you. You must learn how to tell the true prophets from the false. You need to learn to be a talent scout.

If you interviewed a large number of people about their major regrets in life, I'll bet several would tell you they made choices that they regretted because they got bad legal, financial, or career advice. People can mislead you in a variety of ways, intentionally or otherwise, for a variety of reasons, and with a variety of motives. You'll need to have keen command of your validation skills to sift through the large amount of chaff that may come your way.

Legendary football coach Woody Hayes said that when a quarterback threw a pass there were three outcomes…and two of them were bad. With respect to soliciting ideas, there are four outcomes and three of them are bad. We:

- Involve right people but do not listen to them.

- Involve wrong people and make choices based on what they say.

- Fail to involve someone who could have helped us to make a better choice.

- *Involve right people and listen to them.*

While some of the biggest mistakes made by governments, corporations, or individuals are a result of involving the wrong people, on a more pedestrian level, organizations can suffer from the dysfunctional practice of trying to involve too many people. The result is that twenty people attend a meeting when only five should be there. That is a recipe for failure.

The skill of leveraging is a key ingredient of success that you can actually improve. Success takes a certain amount of innate intelligence and a certain amount of luck. There's not much you can do to improve your IQ, and almost nothing you can do to change your luck. But you most certainly can learn to improve your utilization of other people and, simultaneously, make better use of your own unique talents.

In your work, while you are utilizing the talents of others, they are also capitalizing on yours. It is a reciprocal process. I use you for a sanity check and you use me. You listen to my dress rehearsal and then use me to explore alternatives. You get some help; you give some. We all leverage each other.

At least we should. However, most of us barely scratch the surface when it comes to fully leveraging the talents of others. In fact, when it comes to this skill, most people I know would score about 25 on a 100-point scale.

As I have pointed out, the potential benefits you can achieve from mastering this skill are staggering. You can make better decisions, save time, increase your ability to sell ideas, increase the chances that a good idea will be effectively implemented, decrease risks, or discover opportunities.

If you are a competitive person, the argument for taking better advantage of the talents of the people around you is even more compelling. Just imagine that some of your competitors for top-level jobs are as smart as you are and work as hard as you do. Suppose they are identical to you in all respects but one: You have figured out how to leverage your talents by taking full advantage of the different ways people you know can help you. Who is going to win?

Sometimes the process of leveraging other people requires significant amounts of time; sometimes it takes only a little. It can be fun and easy or it can be torture. Most of the time, however, leveraging is an endlessly enriching and gratifying journey. As you travel through life, you never know whom you're going to get help from or how people are going to help you.

Some people develop these skills into an art form, and watching them operate is like watching Michael Jordan play basketball. Their flight is high and their aim is true. They then can end up with the same point of view of Picasso, who said the whole secret to his success as an artist was his skill in plagiarizing.

Validating

People who make better choices are skilled in validating.

Validating external information. We're all inundated with information, much of which is irrelevant, misleading, distorted, incomplete, or just plain incorrect. Therefore, we all have to strive to increase our skills in learning how to verify, validate, check and double-check the information we receive, and on which we base important choices.

Checking on our internal maps. We all make choices on the basis of our mental maps. These mental maps are either an accurate or inaccurate representation of the real world.

Let me give two quick example of how validation works. Larry Pickering was promoted and had to relocate his family from Chicago to New Jersey. He came to New Jersey and made the rounds with a real estate agent while he was staying in a local motel. When he found a house he liked, instead of taking the word of the real estate agent about the length of his commute, he got up early one morning, went to the house, drove to the office at the time he would normally leave for work.

Bob Goodpasture hired a contractor to build a house not far from where Bob was living. On regular basis, he went to check on the progress to see if everything was going according to plan. On one such trip, he found the layout of the rooms was incorrect and he caught the error in time to have it corrected. On important issues, the best course of action is to check and double check.

VALIDATING EXTERNAL INPUT: SORTING THROUGH JUNK MAIL

We are flooded with an abundance of information. Tomorrow, before you read the paper, you already know that some content is inaccurate, imprecise, irrelevant, or inconsequential; you also know that some is valid and useful.

When you ask any top-level executive how many news reports about his or her company are 100 percent accurate, what do you think the answer will be? People know from personal experience about distortions that occur in the press. The paradox is that these same people will read something about another company and accept what is written as true. Sometimes it is like one part of the brain is not connected.

When I read the paper or watch TV, I often think of a friend of mine who was a captain in the army. He got into an ugly fight with one of his lieutenants in the officer's club. My friend was extremely drunk and, without a doubt, disorderly. The next day he was ordered to report to the Colonel, who gave him a severe dressing down and, as punishment, ordered him to give twenty-five percent of his next month's pay to the church of his choice. My friend chose the church he had attended during his childhood in Galveston.

A week later, the local paper ran a story praising this noble, clean living, God-fearing Christian son of Galveston who had so generously remembered his former church.

Because we're all deluged with half-truths and outright falsehoods, we must be vigilant in evaluating and assessing the information we receive, and be careful not to make decisions based on any single piece of information. According to a certain media critic, one of the country's leading newspapers ('renowned for its probity) separates the wheat from the chaff and prints the chaff. So it's up to us to find the wheat.

Tomorrow, you may attend a meeting. Before you go, be aware that some of the people attending will not know what they are talking about. Some can't be trusted, and some are inexperienced or don't communicate well. The competent individuals are going to put forth propositions that are in their best interests, not necessarily in your best interests or those of the company. It's your job to sort through the junk mail. Know the capabilities and hidden agendas of your colleagues, and make sure to validate their statements before you act on them.

The consequences of failing to validate information are amply demonstrated throughout history. Tragedies about those who act on information that is incorrect or incomplete are ubiquitous.

INCORRECT INFORMATION

Bernard Baruch, in his book *My Own Story*, writes how he lost a fortune by investing in the American Spirits Company without taking time to ensure that his information was correct:

> "At the time I bought its stock, American Spirits was still the largest manufacturer and distributor of liquor in America. Hearing that a move was brewing to combine American with three other large liquor concerns, which would have just about bottled up the whiskey business in the United States, I put everything I had into American Spirits stock. News of the forthcoming consolidation was made public
>
> But, contrary to expectations, the fizz went out of American Spirits stock.
>
> It was one of the quickest losses I ever have suffered, and the largest loss in proportion to my total fortune...My course violated every sound rule of speculation. I acted on unverified information after superficial investigation and, like thousands of others before and since, got just what my conduct deserved."

INCOMPLETE INFORMATION

Judging or making choices based on incomplete information is like playing cards without a full deck. You can't win. For instance, you've probably known friends who have undergone a divorce. When you get one person's view you become full of righteous indignation at the other party. Then you get the other half of the story and only then do you have the complete picture of the situation.

In another case, one sales organization with which I worked held meetings for its managers every year. In addition to managers, it was traditional for the company's president to attend, as well. This president had a bad habit. During these meetings, he would come into brief contact with the managers, chatting over a drink with one, sitting next to another at lunch. Based on these brief conversations, he would come to a firm conclusion that a given person was great, average, or worthless. This created incredible problems for the national sales manager, when the recommendations he later made about salary increases, bonuses, or promotions were often rejected by the president if they didn't synch with his opinion of the managers involved.

Fortunately, the national sales manager was a courageous individual. Before one of the meetings, he entered the president's office and, in a politically correct manner, asked him not to attend. He said: "You can't help yourself. When you socialize with people you make snap decisions about them. I have much more data about our employees than you. I know more about their performance and potential than you, and when you get into the act, bad decisions are made too many times." To the credit of the president, he agreed, and decided not to attend the meeting.

This story is not an anomaly. With surprising regularity, executives in high-level positions come to invalid conclusions about employees in their organizations based on very limited data.

If you get expert at validating, you will experience two major consequences:

1. The percentage of good decisions you make will increase over time, based on your ability to find better and better ways to be more confident that your mental map accurately reflects reality.

2. If you are perceived as an individual who makes good decisions, your personal credibility will increase, which in turn will increase the quality of information you receive, which will increase the quality of your decisions.

Validation can play a big role in the success of individuals in many different ways. When you think of Bob Hope's success, do you wonder how validation helped him? Hope had the insight to realize that while he could deliver funny lines, he would need outstanding writers to provide him with material. So, early in his career, he hired 10 gag writers. Each would work independently, and then would reconvene to finalize the weekly TV show.

Hope would assemble the group in a room and ask each writer to discuss his material. If the other writers laughed, the monologue passed the test.

WHAT YOU KNOW THAT ISN'T SO: RECONCILING THE MAP AND THE TERRITORY

"It's amazing what ordinary people can do if they set out without preconceived notions." Charles F. Kettering

Are you familiar with the idea of map and territory? The famous Polish Count Korzybski, father of general semantics, coined it. In Korzybski's reading of human understanding, we walk around with an internal map comprising preconceived notions that can differ in significant ways from the corresponding territory, or the real world. That is, our internal conception of the way things are can fail to match reality. When our internal maps are faulty, we are not objective and we can make bad decisions.

Most of our internal maps include a collection of biases, prejudices, and obsolete ideas. Many of us tend to make mistakes because we think our way is the only way. Every day we get tangled in the jungle of semantics. We have fantasies about how our managers, subordinates, or spouses should behave, we draw firm conclusions from loose data and chronically underestimate or overestimate variables that can help or hurt us. We act on the basis of obsolete maps.

If you make a decision or take an action and things proceed as expected with no surprises, this means that your mental map was more or less in sync with the territory. When the maps don't match the territory, the opposite is true. When you make a recommendation you think is clear-cut and it's summarily rejected, you have a problem with your map. If you do something you think will make your spouse ecstatically happy, but instead he or she gets irritated, you have a map problem. If you invest in a stock that should increase and it doesn't, or when you deliver a sensational performance and receive no praise, you have a map problem.

When the map and territory are in agreement, we communicate, understand, influence, and make decisions easily, confidently, and with minimal stress. When the map and reality don't correspond, the opposite is true: We are inefficient, ineffective, make poor decisions, and endure unnecessary stress. Therefore, adjusting your internal maps to match the territory can have an enormous impact.

From time to time, we can all benefit from checking to see whether any of the following defective maps are currently stored in our mental capacities.

TYPES OF DEFECTIVE MAPS

One kind of mistake we may make is the result of the meaning we attach to certain words. Let us take the word "*island*." If you surveyed a large number of people, I assume the majority of them would think that an island is a small body of land surrounded by water. Many years ago, the cabinet of the U.S. government was certainly under that impression.

During the Kennedy administration, the cabinet met to consider an invasion of Cuba. It became apparent to one individual that most of the cabinet members thought of Cuba the island as a small piece of land like Bermuda and they were, accordingly, assuming that the proposed invasion would result in a quick and easy victory. General Shoup, Commandant of the Marine Corps, pointed out that Cuba was not a small piece of real estate, but 800 miles long—about the width of Texas.

I have friends—a married couple—who were born and raised on Long Island. The husband was in education and was offered an attractive opportunity to become dean of a college in New Jersey. When he told his wife he wanted to accept the job, she cried for a week. In her mind—in her mental map—New Jersey was endless miles of oil refineries, interstate highways, and pig farms. Imagine her delight when her map was corrected. She arrived at her new home in New Jersey surrounded by rolling green hills and beautiful countryside.

This incident reminds me of a famous psychiatrist who said that, based on his experience, the biggest problem most people have is not what they don't know, but what they know that isn't so.

SITUATIONALLY INAPPROPRIATE PERCEPTIONS

It's one thing to recognize when an internal perception is simply wrong or no longer viable. It gets more problematic when the problem with your map is not that it's absolutely incorrect, but wrong for the situation. Objectivity requires situational awareness.

I'm aware of a major flaw in my map whenever I go to London. Although I know that cars travel on the left side of the street, I'm not able to translate this knowledge into safely crossing the street. I've repeatedly looked in all possible directions and thought I understood where the traffic was coming from yet stepped headlong into the path of a speeding taxi. So far, I haven't been able to correct my map. But I have found an alternative. Whenever I need to cross a London street, I wait until I view locals waiting to cross in the same direction. When they proceed, I follow, to which I credit the fact that I'm still alive today.

WHAT TO DO WHEN THINGS GO WRONG

When I'm frustrated, perplexed or when things aren't turning out the way I expect them to, I make a habit of reevaluating my maps, particularly my view of other people's maps.

When I began consulting, my very first assignment was to work with an engineering firm that had a formidable reputation in the steam generation business, Babcock & Wilcox, or B&W.

B&W hired 100 mechanical engineers from college campuses. After the candidates were interviewed on campus, the more qualified ones were invited to visit corporate headquarters. The standard program at the home office included being evaluated by a head shrinker, and I was one of them.

I'd interview each applicant and give him a short battery of tests. After formulating an opinion, I'd contact one person to review my findings. I would then discuss the applicant's intelligence, emotional maturity, drive, interpersonal skills and potential among other criteria. On one hand, this went very smoothly. I felt confident because I'd been doing this kind of work for four years in graduate school, and interviewing college graduates was simple compared with interviewing patients entering a mental institution.

However, as the first week progressed, something bothered me. At first, I couldn't put my finger on it. Then I realized that when I had finished my summary of the candidate's strengths and weaknesses, along with a recommendation about hiring, the person to whom I was conveying the report seemed to be bored and disinterested.

What was happening was almost the complete opposite of what I expected. (Like when you work hard and expect a pat on the back and instead you get some heavy criticism.)

I pondered this and, one morning while I was shaving, I identified the problem. My contact, an engineer, wanted me to give him a numerical recommendation. He hoped, expected, and wanted me to be able to identify the ten traits that were correlated with good performance and then calibrate each of these ten traits on a ten-point scale, resulting in a score from 0 to 100.

Once I understood their interests and corrected my map, I solved the problem. I was at fault for not meeting their needs, so I perfected my plan.

After my next interview I called my contact and said, "Seventy-four," and hung up. After the next appointment, I called and gave my complete report, "Forty-five." The last person interviewed was really first-rate, so I picked up the phone, said, "Ninety-three," and hung up. In three days, I was a living legend.

HINTS FOR IMPROVING YOUR MAPS

In my experience, I've found that there are several simple ways to help your mental preconceptions track with reality.

Be aware of your limitations. Actively question your maps and try to keep an open mind. I have the habit of always assuming that my map is limited and that I frequently lack significant information. I continually seek out people who have the right information. Another helpful trick is to consciously recognize the limits of your knowledge and objectivity by routinely using such phrases as "in my experience," "based on the information I have," "in my opinion," and "as far as I know."

When something goes wrong, when you are surprised, when there is a gap between what you expected would happen and what actually happens, reflect to determine if there is a map problem. Instead of feeling sorry for yourself, blaming someone else, finding a scapegoat, or making excuses, revisit the situation to determine if an assumption or bias is to blame. When things are not working out as I expect them to, I often revisit the map/territory issue to see what I might be missing, misinterpreting, or overlooking.

POINTS TO REMEMBER

The key to improving your objectivity is to integrate two skills: validating external information and verifying the accuracy of maps in your head, enabling you to make choices based on facts.

Validation is at the core of one of the most important tasks of high-level managers: putting the right people in the right jobs. Too often, millions of dollars can be lost because senior managers in an organization arrive at conclusions about individuals based on incomplete or inaccurate information. As it's obviously worth the time and effort to hire good people, executives need ways to: (1) validate the facts of a person's track record, and (2) check to ensure that biases are not tarnishing their judgment.

Developing accurate maps that accurately reflect reality has many positive outcomes, including reducing unnecessary frustration and stress and improving your credibility and judgment. An important side effect is that it also helps you know who to trust. When people don't do these things (i.e., are unaware of the limitations of their maps) I take what they say with a grain of salt.

Assessing Risk/Reward

In this chapter we will be talking about risk in the broadest sense of the term. The nature of risk varies tremendously from one situation to another. You might take a career risk by moving to another company. You might find yourself in a situation where you are in conflict with higher-level people and are trying to figure out the best course of action. You may run the risk of being misunderstood, which is a communication risk. There are times when you debate with yourself whether or not you have too much to lose and not enough to gain when you tell someone the unvarnished truth.

Successful people have a knack for sizing up the situation. And because every situation is unique, there is no set formula or rigid set of rules that apply to all situations.

Not only do situations vary, there is also a wide range of possible outcomes. The degree of risk can be very high, very low, or someplace in-between. You can take a risk, make a mistake, and easily recover from it or, at the other extreme, you can make mistakes that are career limiting.

When you master the common sense problem-solving model, you will be: (1) asking questions, which are often risk relevant; (2) involving others, which often results in your finding risks that you had not thought about; and (3) validating—being sure you base decisions on rock-solid information. (It is also essential to be able to determine who to trust and that will be discussed in the chapter on trust.)If you do those things well, you can dramatically reduce the chances of taking inappropriate risks.

As a final step in ratcheting up your risk-taking skills to the highest level, there are very important lessons to be learned by using successful mutual fund managers as role models. If a fund manager plays it too safe, they miss big opportunities; if they are too aggressive, their funds can sustain unnecessary and significant losses. Four abilities define the successful ones:

- They have a balanced approach to risk taking.

- They learn to cut their losses.

- They are good at predicting behavior.

- Their sense of timing sets them apart from the crowd.

THEY HAVE A BALANCED APPROACH TO RISK TAKING

Their balanced approach to risk/reward is well illustrated by the research conducted many years ago by David McClelland, a Harvard professor. He devoted his life to the study of the achievement motive. In a very cleverly designed experiment, McClelland had grade school children play ring toss, a game very much like horseshoes. He gave the children a number of plastic rings and asked them to toss them to encircle a wooden pole. He did not tell the children how far away they should stand from the pole.

The first group stood about 10 feet away. They wanted to take on high risk, to heighten the glory of the potential reward. These are the high rollers—the riverboat gamblers the cowboys who should probably end up joining Gambler's Anonymous.

The second group comprised ultraconservatives who were risk averse. They stood close to the pole and carefully placed one ring after another immediately on top of it. They succeeded in fulfilling the task, but experienced only modest rewards.

The final group stood somewhere in-between. They took a position on the floor that would make the task challenging, and thus rewarding, without making the task too easy or too difficult. The successful mutual fund managers would undoubtedly have been in this group that avoided the two extremes. In Aristotle's terms, virtue is the path between two vices; cautious, but not too cautious, and more than willing to take sensible risks. In a word, balanced.

Gordon Moore became a billionaire from his Intel stock. In discussing the strategy for developing the computer chip that revolutionized the industry, he described how the right strategy was developed: "The key was the right degree of complexity. Too easy, you get competition too soon. Too hard, you run out of money before you get it done."

Warren Buffett made a similar point. He said, "I don't try to jump over 7 foot bars: I look around for 1 foot bars that I can step over."

THEY LEARN TO CUT THEIR LOSSES

As anyone who has been involved in buying and selling stocks knows, a cardinal rule of investing is to cut your losses. This is another of the hallmarks of the mutual fund managers who have the best track records. The reason it is such an important rule is that stock selector's error rate is quite high. Edmund C. Lynch, cofounder of Merrill Lynch, said that if he made a decision fast, he was correct sixty percent of the time. If he made it carefully, he was right seventy percent of the time. (I can't believe he told his customers he expected to be wrong 30 to 40% of the time.)

What is the prime application of this maxim for business managers? It has to do primarily with personnel decisions. As there's a high error rate in selecting stocks, there's also a high error rate in hiring and promoting people. If a person had a nearly perfect record, they could quit their job, devote their time to recruitment, and make a fortune. However, most managers make more mistakes than they would like to admit. What distinguishes the best managers from the crowd is that they are quicker to cut their losses or to correct mistakes made by others.

In my view, Alfred Sloan was one of the greatest managers/businessmen in U.S. industrial history. He ran the nations largest company, General Motors, over a period spanning the depression and World War II.

In his memoirs, *My Forty Years with General Motors*, Alfred Sloan reports on major lessons he had learned. "First, I think we have lacked the courage in dealing with the weaknesses in personnel. We know the weaknesses exist, we tolerate them and finally after tolerating them an abnormal length of time, we made the change and then regret that we have not acted before."

Here is one of the leading figures of all time who ran a premier company through good times and adversity, and the primary learning he gained was how serious the consequences were of not cutting your losses when you have people in the wrong jobs.

THEY ARE GOOD AT PREDICTING BEHAVIOR

John Maynard Keynes, the world famous economist, was also an astute investor. He made an eye-opening observation that you may want to remember. He said that picking a stock was like being a judge at a beauty contest, if your purpose as a judge were to pick the lady the other judges would select.

Hundreds of millions of dollars are bet by hedge fund and mutual fund managers based on predictions. Does that surprise you? When Louis Gerstner took over IBM, these managers bet substantial sums on the belief that he could turn the company around. When Bob Nardelli left GE to run Home Depot the same thing happened.

George Soros and other hedge fund managers bet millions of dollars based on their predictions regarding whether governments are likely to raise or lower interest rates.

◆   ◆   ◆

An excellent example of the importance of making accurate predictions has to do with the Marshall Plan. After World War II, some staffers in the U.S. State Department had come up with a novel plan designed to avoid the depression that followed most wars. Quite simply, the plan was for the U.S. to give financial support to the European countries so they could get back on their feet economically. They wanted to call it the Truman Plan. When they suggested this to the President, he rejected the idea of using his name. He sensed that many members of Congress were hostile and would vote down a good idea because his name was associated with it. He recommended a different name: The Marshall Plan. If the original label has been used and Congress had defeated the measure, the world could very well have been worse off today.

THEIR SENSE OF TIMING SETS THEM APART FROM THE CROWD

The rule of investing in stocks is to buy low and sell high. That implies that the investor should have a great sense of timing. One of the deans of investing, John Templeton, insisted the best time to buy was when everyone was pessimistic.

A high percentage of middle and high-level executives are action oriented. They believe in the quotation, "He who hesitates is lost". Their have to feel that they are under pressure to get closure, to decide and move on. The effective risk taker bases decision on the nature of the situation. In some situations, hesitation is the best course of action.

Bob Wilson spent his career with Johnson & Johnson (J&J), retiring as Senior Vice Chairman of the Board. He played a dominant role in building the pharmaceutical business of Johnson & Johnson. The major indigenous American companies Lilly, Upjohn, and Squibb started around 1860. Johnson & Johnson didn't get serious about the drug business until around 1960. Of the companies that had a 100 year head start, only one (Lilly) has survived, whereas J&J, at the time of this writing, ranks fourth in the world. Wilson was one of a handful of executives who made that happen. He always enjoyed paraphrasing the ad about no wine before its time by saying, "No decision before its time."

Under what circumstances did Wilson find hesitation to be the best strategy?

1. There is no compelling reason to make the decision immediately.

2. Now is not the right time, and it is very much to your advantage to control the timing of the decision.

3. The problem may resolve itself without an intervention.

4. Some external event you can neither predict nor control may be so important that it can be decision determining, so the wisest course is to hold steady and see how events unfold.

The comments I have made about Bob Wilson have also been made about Robert Rubin, a former partner at Goldman and Sachs and Secretary of the Treasury under Bill Clinton. As reported in *Fortune*, "Part of Rubin's approach to decisions in the Treasury was to put them off as long as possible…Rubin called it getting that one last fact or well-judged opinion that might make a decision the right one. Rubin's first question would often be, 'How much time do we have before we have to decide?'"

When M. Gupta was elected to be the managing director of McKinsey (one of the world's most prestigious consulting firms), he insisted that one of his major strengths was his ability to figure out when it was best to delay taking action. He insisted many problems had a way of resolving themselves without any intervention.

I think Rudy Giuliani, the former mayor of New York City, who wrote a book entitled *Leadership*, made the best summation. He devotes an entire chapter to this subject. He said:

> One of the trickiest elements of decision making is working out not what, but when…I never make up my mind until I have to…Many are tempted to decide an issue simply to end the discomfort of indecision. However, the longer you have to make a decision, the more mature and well reasoned that decision should be.

Individuals like Wilson, Rubin, Gupta, and Giuliani are rare. They are the exception rather than the rule. The kind of procrastination that leads to paralysis by analysis resulting in missing opportunities is much more common. In these cases, the decision maker unrealistically wants more and more information.

This type of procrastination was in a remarkable three-page cartoon run by *The New Yorker* magazine. The cartoon had a series of drawings of a man walking in the woods. He came across a small pond. The center of the pond was bubbling as if there was a spring. The pond spoke to the man and said, "Jump in and you will have eternal youth." The man was startled (I guess ponds had never talked to him before) and he jumped behind a large tree. When he regained his composure, he cautiously stuck his head out and asked the brook, "What do you mean by Eternal Youth?" The pond refused to give him the definition he sought, but instead just repeated its first offer: "Jump in and you will have Eternal Youth." The man then asked the brook for reference. He wanted a list of people who had jumped into the pond. Again, the pond gave him no reassurance. Instead, it once again said, "Jump in and you will have eternal youth." Well, you could tell the man was somewhat intrigued, but he still wanted more information, so he asked the pond how this might affect his 401K, his stock options, and his pension plan. The bubbling stopped and the pond grew quiet. The man returned to his house and when his wife asked him if anything interesting had happened on his walk, he told her, "No."

I have often thought of this cartoon because it captures the essence of timid corporate bureaucrats who suffer from paralysis by analysis. They fail to recognize that there is a point of diminishing returns—a moment when it is a waste of time, energy, and money to delay a decision any longer.

ADDITIONAL THOUGHTS ON RISK TAKING

The conventional view of risk taking is a gross oversimplification, as if it is a straightforward and fairly simple process of weighing the reward or the opportunity in comparison to the risk or possible downside. It is much more complex, because each situation is unique. In one situation, Factor A is the most critical variable, whereas in another situation Factor A is not decision determining.

For example, in some situations success will depend on figuring out the odds of winning or losing. In other situations, the odds are well known and the overriding issue is the ability to predict behavior. The examples below are intended to show just a few of the permutations and combinations of how decision determining factors very greatly, depending on the situation.

When it comes to risk taking, there is no formula; there is no rulebook.

ASSESSING THE ODDS

An essential skill of the effective risk taker is well illustrated by a neat story about Warren Buffett, who is known as the "Sage of Omaha." Warren Buffett has become renowned for his investment track record and his humor. For several years, he has been listed as one of the wealthiest people in the United States. He was playing golf with some friends at Pebble Beach in California when they ventured a bet. They were willing to pay him $20,000 if he made a hole in one during the three days of their vacation. If he didn't make a hole in one, he had to pay them $10.

How would the majority react to this kind of proposition? They would ask two questions: "What do I have to win?" and, "What do I have to lose?" They have little to lose and a great deal to gain. These are the same two questions asked by people who play lotteries. The answer: "Go For It!"

I think this is a good example of how people can be superficial or slipshod in their analyses. Buffett was more thorough. Buffett didn't take the bet because he asked a third question (the decision-determining question),

"What are my chances of losing?" The answer: His chances of losing were very close to 100 percent.

Many individuals who invest in stocks make serious mistakes by taking risks on assumptions about the potential reward.

The following excerpt is from Peter Lynch's book "*One Up on Wall Street*".

> If you're considering a stock on the strength of some specific product that a company makes, the first thing to find out is: What effect will the success of the product have on the company's bottom line? Back in February of 1988, investors got very enthused about RetinA, a skin cream made by Johnson & Johnson. The newspapers loved this story and headline writers called it the antiaging cream and the wrinkle fighter. You would have thought that Johnson & Johnson has discovered the Fountain of Youth.

The stock jumped $8 a share, adding $1.4 billion to the company's market cap, but the sales of RetinA increased the earnings of the company minimally.

Too many times people have taken risks on the basis of very limited information: They make a bet based on a fantasy rather than a realistic assessment of the magnitude of the opportunity.

In other situations, the odds are not the primary issue. Take the example of the professional poker player. Everyone knows that when the deck has 52 cards, the odds of drawing a spade are 1 out of 4; the odds of drawing a face card are 4 out of 13. The players who win are better at making accurate predictions, for example, figuring out if the opponent is bluffing. This skill was captured in the Kenny Roger's song: "You have to know when to hold 'em, know when to fold 'em, know when to walk away, know when to run."

BEING CONSCIOUS OF THE POTENTIAL LOSS

Fos Whitlock was one of the top three executives of Johnson & Johnson. He asked me to talk to his son, Brant. Brant was about to graduate from college and was obsessed with the idea that he had the potential to be a professional golfer. Fos asked me to meet with Brant, obviously hoping that I would steer him toward giving up his dream of being a professional golfer. After seeing Brant, I met with Fos and suggested that he had too much to lose. If Brant were deprived of the chance to see if he had the right stuff to become a pro golfer, he would never know if he could have been successful. He would then hate his father for the rest of his life for depriving him of this opportunity. What was worse: The possibility of risking some money by supporting his son or running the risk of his son's lifelong enmity? To his great credit, Fos did an about-face and made what I think was the right choice.

MANAGING RISK

The next anecdote has two morals: (1) Many times, you will have to figure out the best way to manage a risk; and (2) You can lose when you say the wrong thing to the wrong person at the wrong time. Some years ago, George Squibb, grandson of the founder of Squibb, the pharmaceutical company, had driven to the Squibb Research Center in New Brunswick, New Jersey, with two world-renowned physicians. When Mr. Squibb arrived at the gate, he found that he did not have his employee identification badge. The guard faced a dilemma, because if he allowed someone to drive into the plant without the proper identification he could be fired.

George identified himself as the Vice President of Marketing of the company. What should the guard have said to himself? "If this guy is really an industrial spy, and I let him through the gate, I could be in trouble. If this guy is who he says he is, and I turn him away, I could be in deep trouble. What is the best way to find out if this guy is who he says he is or if he is an imposter?" All he had to do was to let the car through, and then call the receptionist at the administrative center and say that she should expect George Squibb to be signing in shortly. If it were not George Squibb, she would know and refuse him entrance. The question the guard needed to ask himself had to do with how he could manage the risk.

What did the guard do? The guard said, "Of course, and I am Mickey Mouse," and refused to allow the car onto the grounds. It was a career-limiting move. Not only did the guard fail to ask the right questions, he should have easily won the championship trophy in the annual foot-in-mouth contest.

ANALYZING THE CONSEQUENCES OF ALL OUTCOMES

The thirty-sixth president was Lyndon Baines Johnson, often known as LBJ. When Jack Kennedy was nominated as the Democratic Party's presidential candidate, he offered the VP slot to Lyndon Johnson. LBJ had mixed emotions.

Johnson was a very proud individual. He was well aware that vice presidents were relegated to menial tasks, and he had been accustomed to being in the spotlight as the Senate Majority Leader. Confronted with the prospects of being offered the vice-presidential slot on the ticket, it's not difficult to imagine that Johnson recognized it would be hard for him to be completely objective. His logical course of action was to seek the advice of a trusted friend.

He sought the advice of John Connally, then governor of Texas. Connally did an excellent job of assessing risks and rewards of potential outcomes. He told Johnson he could not decline the vice-presidential candidacy, using this explanation:

> If LBJ refused and JFK lost, everyone would blame it on him.
>
> If he refused and JFK won, his name would be mud.
>
> If he accepted and JFK lost, he would have the best Democratic job in the country as majority leader.
>
> If he accepted and JFK won, LBJ would be next in line for the top job.

There are many examples of people who make bad choices because of a lack of objectivity. In this case, it is reasonable to assume that LBJ was aware that he might err because he was not being objective. He needed a sanity check. He involved the right person an old friend from Texas who was an astute politician and a very logical thinker. In analyzing the problem, Connally demonstrated good foresight in analyzing all possible outcomes.

TAKING THE LONG-RANGE POINT OF VIEW

There are many cases in which you can involve the right people, but you need to ignore their advice. In the 1950s, Merck was undergoing a global expansion. A proposition was made to build a plant in India. Most senior managers were opposed because, in their view, the worst possibility was that in the future, there would be a political upheaval leading to the Indian government taking over the plant. If this were the result, Merck would lose its entire investment.

However, the decision was made to invest in India because the president of Merck, Jack Connor, had a different point of view. His vision was that, over a long period of time, Merck would be able to make substantial profits from the Indian operation. On the other hand, in the worst-case scenario, the company would have lost its entire investment of several million dollars. The questions he posed were: (1) "Can Merck survive the loss of several million?" The answer was, "Of course," and (2) "Does the potential gain outweigh this risk?" The answer was, "Yes."

In thinking through this issue, Jack made a prediction. He predicted that it was highly unlikely that the Indian government would nationalize the plant. His prediction was correct. Furthermore, in assessing the risk, he had a clear appreciation that every year the potential loss was decreased.

In most of these case histories and illustrations, there are multiple lessons to be learned. Certainly, Connor was asking the right questions. He made a prediction about the behavior of the Indian government that turned out to be true. It is also important to note that in his approach to the problem, he did not just focus on the near term, but took the long-range view. Finally, Connor demonstrated one of the qualities of people who have high ego-strength: The herd did not stampede him.

WHEN RISK IS NOT EVEN ON THE RADAR SCREEN

William Henry Harrison, the ninth president of the United States, holds the record for having the shortest tenure of any U.S. president. He served from March 4, 1841, to April 4, 1841; exactly one month. What happened? He gave the longest inaugural speech on record (one hour and forty-five minutes), refusing to wear a hat or coat on a very cold and rainy day. He caught pneumonia and died. He either failed to question the wisdom of his actions—he did not ask the right question—or he asked the right question and came up with the wrong answer. He didn't have enough common sense to get out of the rain. I think it's likely that Harrison was risk obtuse (i.e., one of those individuals who take risks without knowing what they are doing).

WHAT IS THE RIGHT THING TO DO??

Sometimes, the best course of action is to focus on what is right rather than on risk/reward. As a case in point, Bill Weldon was one of a group of about forty J&J executives each responsible for a profit center. This was at a time when policies favoring casual dress were just becoming popular. Many of his contemporaries looked at the issue in terms of risk versus reward. They came to the conclusion that they had nothing to gain and, perhaps, something to lose. Bill thought casual dress was the right thing to do and instituted the policy in his company.

POINTS TO REMEMBER

To improve your skill as an effective risk taker, you should remember the following points.

- Using the Common Sense Problem-Solving Model can help you be a more effective risk-taker.

- Compare yourself with the abilities of the best fund managers who have a balanced approach to risk, discipline themselves to cut their losses, improve in their ability to predict behavior, and develop a sense of timing that sets them apart from the crowd.

Section 2

Three Critical
Interpersonal
Competencies

Building Relationships Based on Mutual Trust

Learning how to earn trust and figuring out who to trust has a huge effect on your ability to get results, to earn a desirable reputation, and to build productive relationships. Trust is, in some respects, simple; you know, for example, if you want to be trusted you should keep your promises. This idea is clear and simple. However, in other ways, trust is highly complex. Most managers who tend to be quiet in meetings don't realize they can unconsciously created trust problems, a point which will be discussed later in this chapter.

The motto of the individual with common sense is, "There is a sucker born every minute, and I am not going to be one."

Trust has different meanings depending on the context or the specific situation. Also, you can trust a person in some ways but not in others. You trust someone because:

- You know where you stand with them.

- You can believe what they tell you.

- You have confidence in them.

- You can confide in them.

- They are on your side; they have your best interests at heart.

- They are consistent and predictable.

- They keep their promises.

(Obviously, each and every one of the above doesn't have to be satisfied in order for there to be some level of trust. Also, the above statements apply to those who trust you.)

In all cases, when someone trusts you in one sense or another, it's because you make them feel secure, make them feel safe, and conversely when you trust someone, you feel secure.

Of course, it is all a matter of degree. Your level of security might be 100% or 0% or someplace in between. It is like a ruler which is painted to show the shades of grey in between black and white : black, dark grey, medium grey, light grey and white.

Trust = security = certainty = low doubt
Lack of trust = insecurity = uncertainty = high doubt

The famous evangelist, Oral Roberts, visited a small town to do a guest sermon at a local church. Roberts came out of his hotel and saw a small boy. He approached the boy and asked for directions to the post office. The child gave him directions, and Roberts, by way of thanks, said: "Tomorrow's Sunday and I'm giving a sermon on how to get to Heaven. Why don't you come?" "No, thank you," the boy said. "How can you know how to get to Heaven if you don't even know how to get to the post office?"

Doubt was created because, in the mind of the boy, if Roberts couldn't figure out something as simple as knowing how to get to the post office, how could he possibly know how to get to heaven?

There are three basic rules about getting and giving trust.

RULE ONE:
DON'T LISTEN TO THE IGUANAS

During World War II, a young recruit was stationed at a remote outpost on an island in the South Pacific. When he first arrived, his master sergeant told him that the island was populated with some funny looking, rather ugly animals called iguanas. Watch duty was a lonely affair, tedious, redundant and solitary. "After a while, you'll start talking to the iguanas," said the master sergeant. "Don't worry; it's a phase we all go through. And after a while, you'll start hearing them talk to you. Don't worry about that, either. But if you start listening to them, that's when you worry."

A lot of good people have made a lot of bad decisions because they listened to the iguanas—that is, they listened to the wrong people and took action based on what those people said. When you are deciding whether or not to trust someone, make sure you're not listening to one of the two main types of iguanas:

A Player	**Iguanas**
Don't take a position unless they know what they are talking about	Uninhibited by their own ignorance
Avoid jargon	Like jargon and buzzwords
See the gray	See issues as black or white
Make a thorough and complete analysis	React on the basis of superficial information
Don't accept things at face value	Don't adequately question people's opinions or facts
Don't argue with you when you know more than they do	Debate with people who are better informed or more knowledgeable
Cut to the crux of the problem	Become entrenched at the periphery of the problem

IGUANA TYPE #1:
YOU ARE NOT SURE THEY KNOW WHAT THEY ARE TALKING ABOUT

You feel insecure when you sense a person does not know what they are talking about. Their argument is not logical, their analysis is incomplete, or they don't have good answers to your questions. Sometimes people just aren't smart enough to know what they don't know. They may be gullible and believe whatever they have read or been told. Or they may be limited, either in their experiences and knowledge, or in their viewpoint and perspective.

The following charts should help you detect Type #1 iguanas and discern the difference between them and the "A Players," people you can really trust.

Since time is one of the most inelastic of resources and is too precious to waste, you shouldn't waste time with iguanas. If possible, avoid them as much as you can.

IGUANA TYPE #2:
YOU SUSPECT THEIR MOTIVES

As a general guideline, it is prudent to follow the advice of Warren Buffett who said: "Don't ask a barber if you need a haircut."

You have to be aware of all the different agendas which people have. There are people who will tell you only what they think you want to hear. Others are self-serving and want to manipulate you. Some people are natural-born liars. They have lost the ability to tell the difference between lying and telling the truth.

RULE TWO:
FIGURE OUT HOW YOU CAN AVOID CREATING
TRUST PROBLEMS

Unintentionally, all of us create trust problems for ourselves. It is incumbent on each of us to understand the type of trust problems which we might create and find a way to make appropriate adjustments. Which type of trust problem do you create?

Suppose you are one of the most likable people around. That can be a major strength, but it can also be a weakness. In trying to win the approval of others, individuals like you can create trust problems.

The weekly calendar of one such person, who we will call Gary, follows. On Monday he'd agree with one person about something, that the walls should be painted blue, let's say. On Tuesday, someone else would say that green was a better color and Gary would agree. On Wednesday...Well, you get the point. In effect, the person who got his or her way was the one who got in the last word. Shortly, most people mistrusted him because they learned his agreement meant nothing. Unfortunately, he had to be demoted. The level of trust you establish can be seriously impaired if you have an overwhelming desire to win the popularity contest.

Suppose you tend to be one of the quieter people in a team meeting. Just when you are ready to interject an idea, someone else mentions it. You choose not to say anything. By not contributing much, you may think of yourself as congenial and cooperative. But, others may think of you as unwilling to take a stand. Since they do not know where you stand on issues, you create doubt and they feel insecure. Quiet people can create big problems for themselves.

Suppose you are one of the most ambitious people in your work group, a hard charger who gets things done. What trust problems can that create for you? People may feel you are willing to put their careers in jeopardy to further your ambitions. You may have to work hard to control your ambition to avoid creating counterproductive insecurity.

Suppose you are one of the smartest people in your part of the company. Is it possible that people feel insecure because you can tear their ideas to shreds? IQ can be—and frequently is—a liability as well as an asset. Some of the cleverest executives I know are careful to hide their intelligence rather than flaunt it.

Suppose you are the overly enthusiastic type, the perennial optimist. You don't just see the half-empty glass as being half full; you run around the room with the glass containing a few drops of water proclaiming you have found the fountain of youth and are looking for the right packaging. Because you are prone to exaggeration, people do not pay attention to you, do not take you seriously, and do not believe you.

Suppose you are a very strong-willed, forceful person who frightens people. Your subordinates will not stand up to you and they will not tell you when you are about to make a mistake. This is, in short, a recipe for disaster.

How consistent are you? The best leaders—those who are most trusted—are those who are consistent in giving direction. Consistency works reciprocally. The best subordinates are consistent, giving their leaders a sense of interpersonal security.

The leaders or subordinates who drive everyone crazy, and who get no trust from their coworkers, are the ones who are constantly changing their minds. Take the manager who walks into your office and says, "We're going to go to Chicago for our annual meeting." So you make a plan to go to Chicago. Two weeks later, he walks back in and says, "Well, I've decided it would be better if we went to Atlanta." So you grumble, but you think, well, OK, everyone has the right to change their mind once in a while, and you cancel all the Chicago arrangements and you make new arrangements for Atlanta. Just about the time you hang up the phone with the last person you need to talk to in Atlanta, the boss waltzes back in and says, "You know, I've been thinking, Detroit is a much better place." Obviously, by this time you're completely fed up and de-motivated. The next time your boss asks you to do something, you're probably going to wait a while to get started, because you don't trust him to make and stick to a plan.

We all have encountered all of these types of people. We are keenly aware of the kinds of behavior that can make us wary of others, but we are generally far less aware of what we might be doing that creates trust problems.

What is your personal trust problem? What can you do about it?

THE COMPLEXITY AND IRRATIONALITY OF TRUST

Many of the subjects we have discussed are logical and rational. You trust people who are predictable and consistent, who do their homework, and so forth. However, from time to time, you will see another side of trust, the irrational side. The following are some stories taken from my experience. They illustrate how everyone has his own highly subjective and often irrational yardsticks which are used to determine who is trustworthy.

Example #1.

People often need to reassure themselves about your trustworthiness in irrational ways. A number of years ago I worked with a man who kept a cigar humidor on his desk. I smoked cigars and also a pipe at that time. Every time I went into this man's office, he took a cigar out of his humidor, cut it, lit it, and handed it to me. Now, while this was a standard ritual for him with me—it happened every time I walked in there—it was something he did with no one else in the organization.

Four or five years later, I found out why. He was born in Malaysia. For some reason, he was taught not to trust anyone who smokes a pipe. I finally understood that this man wanted to trust me but couldn't if I was smoking a pipe. He couldn't get rid of his prejudices. Instead, he gave me a cigar before I could take my pipe out of my pocket!

Example #2.

On a plane, before the collapse of the Berlin wall, I was flying from Frankfurt to Berlin. I was seated next to a German who spoke fluent English. He was interested in American politics and was very well informed. During our conversation, he told me he thought Secretary of State George Schultz was to be trusted because he was trained as an engineer. "Engineers are too stupid to be devious," he said.

Example #3.

My son, Tom, lived in France for a few years. He has a natural linguistic ability and, over time, became exceptionally fluent in French. Repeatedly, coworkers and others would compliment him. "Your French is excellent," they'd say. And my rather modest son would thank them, but he thought they were just being nice and didn't believe a word of it.

One day, however, he was asked to meet the Managing Director of his firm over coffee. This executive had the reputation of never saying anything nice; he was a tough-minded, serious no nonsense kind of guy. During the meeting, he told my son that his French was terrific. This time, Tom truly believed it.

Example #4.

Once a professor from Cornell University and I teamed up to conduct a three day training program. A participant approached me during a break and said he thought both of us seemed pretty smart, but he trusted me more because the other guy had long hair. I gathered that during the lecture he listened to what I had to say, but he tuned out my colleague because of his appearance.

◆　　　◆　　　◆

The level of trust has a major impact on many organization issues such as:

- Decision-Making

- Communications

- Teamwork

- Criterion for promotion

- Superior-subordinate relationships

DECISION-MAKING

Suppose top management has to make a major decision. Suppose the stakes are high, there is considerable uncertainty, and most senior people are not in agreement. What happens then?

In some cases, the person who makes the final decision has strong convictions and trusts her intuition and/or experience. But suppose the person with the final authority has no preconceived notions and does not have a fixed position. What happens then? These tough decisions, often with far reaching implications, are not based on facts; they are based on an interpretation of the facts. The decision depends on who the top dog trusts (i.e., whose opinion is given the greatest weight).

COMMUNICATIONS

Another reason trust has an enormous impact on organizations is the level of trust determines the quality of communications. Honest, open communication helps companies thrive, while guarded, restricted communication can cause insidious problems. Organizations have to work hard to maintain the level of trust that will facilitate open communication. It is not an easy job.

TEAMWORK

Another important organizational goal is to optimize teamwork. There is absolutely no question that the best performing teams have a high level of trust among members.

When Bear Bryant was coaching football at Alabama, he was quoted as saying that he was successful because he had built a team that had a lot of mutual respect for, and trust in, each other. Note that he said he was successful, not because he had been able to recruit the biggest, meanest guys, or because his university had money for the best facilities, or because he himself was a strategic genius, but because trust existed among his players (and coaches).

Look at teams who are losing and you'll often find that the team is divided. Everybody is trying to be a hero, or look good, or do his or her own thing. On the better teams, you're more likely to find people are subordinating their own goals for the sake of the team goal. Instead of trying a difficult, unlikely three point shot that would make me look good if it went in, I pass the basketball to you because you have a better shot, and I trust you to make it.

CRITERION FOR PROMOTION

People often believe that to get promoted all you need is good performance and that no other yardsticks should be used. But the fact is that it's not that clear-cut. Many times, if there are five candidates for a promotion, at least four of them are roughly equal relative to objective performance measures. Who's going to get promoted? The person who engenders the most trust. If you're interested in being promoted, stop and think about whether you're trusted by management. Make trust your primary objective. Why would anybody promote you if they didn't trust you or weren't sure they could?

Every promotion is a prediction. Every prediction is based on a belief. If people believe in you, it means they trust you.

SUPERIOR/SUBORDINATE RELATIONSHIPS: THE TRUST GAP

It would really surprise me if anyone would argue with me about the critical importance of trust. A survey I once read validates this: when 2,615 people were asked to select the most desirable of all leadership characteristics, one trait overshadowed all others: trustworthiness.

Trait	Rank	Percentage of Managers Selecting
Trustworthy	1	83
Competent	2	67
Forwardlooking	3	62
Inspiring	4	58
Intelligent	5	43

(The other 15 traits were selected by less than 40% of the managers.)

But here's the problem. When you ask people how many of their managers have ranked high on the trustworthy scale, you'll find that the answer is only about 25 percent. In other words, if you have had 16 managers, unless you have been very lucky, there are only 4 who you could trust completely. This is what I call the trust gap.

The single biggest factor which creates the trust gap is the rapidity of change.

Dynamic and growing organizations are in a constant state of evolution. These companies hire large numbers of new people, promote people into new work groups, reorganize, and merge with or acquire other companies. What does this high rate of change mean? It means a high percentage of folks are working with people they do not know well. On the other hand, your level of trust is unquestionably related to the length of time you have known someone. (If you list the five people you trust the most, that list will be dominated by people you have known for many years.)

The people who will do the best are those who have perfected their skills so, in new situations, they can dramatically shorten the time it takes them to earn trust and to figure out whom to trust.

POINTS TO REMEMBER

If you look back on your life so far, I'll bet you'll find that some of the worst choices you've made came about because you either:

- Didn't trust someone you should have trusted, or

- Trusted someone you shouldn't have trusted.

Moreover, in a changing world, speed is essential. Individuals who learn how to both (1) determine whom to trust and (2) earn the trust of different kinds of people in a short period of time, will be way ahead of a person who can not master these skills. The most productive working relationships are based on mutual respect and trust.

In addition to having insight into others, you need to develop insight into yourself. Everyone can unconsciously create mistrust. What do you do that either builds or erodes trust? What course corrections do you need to make?

Developing an Other-Oriented Approach to Influence

People with good common sense do the common things uncommonly well. This chapter will give you some helpful hints about improving your ability to influence others, a skill that you use almost every day and one that constantly needs to be refined and perfected. The trick is to shift from being egocentric to being other-oriented. As it turns out, this is a tall order *because we have to learn to do the opposite of what comes naturally.*

I am willing to bet you a substantial sum of money that last month someone said:

- You should meet this person. You will like them.

- You should read this book. You will love it.

- You should see this TV show. You will enjoy it.

The implicit assumption on the part of the person making these statements is that you are like them, making a normal, natural, and unconscious kind of mistake all of us make from time to time. These kinds of interactions clearly illustrate the universal tendency of humans to develop an inefficient perception of reality (i.e., treating people as if they were our psychological twins when they are not). However, in these cases, no great harm is done.

Harm is done when someone is very heavy handed. Think of all the people you know whose parents said to one of their children, you have to go to Timbuktu University. Timbuktu was right for me. Therefore, it is right for you. (The same mistake in logic can be applied to many different aspects of life. For example, you have to come into my business, or join the

69

military service, or marry someone like I married.) In these cases, harm can be done.

The natural, normal tendency to treat people as if they are our psychological twin is a good example of unconscious incompetence. The way to combat unconscious incompetence is through conscious competence, a continuously disciplining of ourselves to treat people as individuals, to be other-oriented As far as I know, the best model to help you move in that direction was developed in the 1960s by a team of two research psychologists, Dr. James W. Taylor and Dr. David W. Merrill. Unlike other models that are hypothetical or speculative, their's is based on rigorous statistical analysis.

According to Taylor and Merrill's findings, each person has a predominant (social) influence style. There are four predominant styles.

The Four Influence Styles

Methodical

Quiet
Reserved
Formal

Competitive

Impatient
Persistent
Decisive

Supportive

Warm
Friendly
Outgoing

Promotional

Enthusiastic
Informal
Dramatic

THE M (METHODICAL) STYLE: DEVELOPING CREDIBILITY THROUGH KNOWLEDGE

I recently bought a DVD player. The salesperson who helped me wasn't someone I particularly liked. I wouldn't have wanted to go out for a beer with him afterwards or work next to him in an office. But I readily bought an expensive set of equipment from him. Why? Because he knew what he was talking about. He established credibility by answering all my questions about the system. He was a typical M.

M's influence others because they are extremely knowledgeable about their subject matter. In the selling field, M's are the ones that sell by virtue of having the best product knowledge. Most M's are logical, organized, and thorough. They believe that the facts speak for themselves. When we are influenced by M's, it's because they come across as true professionals, thoughtful people who are credible because of their command of information. This professional image is the M's greatest advantage in an influence situation.

Maybe you have been assigned to a team. In that team or in your work group, the M's say the least and often have the most to contribute.

But, being an M has its drawbacks. Many M's can be too data centered to the exclusion of other important factors, such as the feelings and emotions of others. Sometimes, because they have command of so much information, it can be hard for M's to reach conclusions. They see all the pro evidence; they see all the con evidence. But, it's hard for them to make decisions.

Most people know that Merck was usually on the list of the most admired companies in the United States. Merck's success was largely attributable to a research organization that had been one of the best in the industry for many years. Research started to really blossom at Merck many years ago under the direction of Dr. Max Tischler.

Max was not a world-class scientist. He was not the inventor of any major product. However, he was a genius at managing scientists. I happened to be present at a meeting which was a great example of his keen understanding of M's. He started the meeting by saying that he did not want them to make any decisions. He was going to make the decisions about what direction they took in the future. (The body language of all the chemists present clearly indicated how relieved they were. It was as if he had just taken a big burden off their shoulders.) He then went on to say that he simply wanted to review the data.

THE P (PROMOTIONAL) STYLE: DEVELOPING CREDIBILITY THROUGH ENTHUSIASM

You might say that the P is the opposite of the M. Instead of trying to influence through facts, the P influences primarily through enthusiasm, through the credibility that comes with conveying great personal sincerity and conviction. Also called The Expressives, P's have the talent of making you feel that they truly believe the message they're sending. Facts never seem to inhibit them.

Many evangelical ministers are probably P's, as are many insurance salespeople. They convince you by the forceful, dramatic ways in which they convey how strongly they feel about your soul's salvation or your family's security. You buy their message or their product because you think, if this person feels so strongly about it, it must be true.

P.T. Barnum would be the epitome of the ultimate P: the showman, the person who loves the dramatic. Teddy Roosevelt and Ronald Reagan are good examples, as well.

When he was 80 years old, Bob Hope, another famous P, was asked why he didn't retire and go fishing. Hope said: "Fish don't applaud!"

Because P's work from the basis of enthusiasm rather than analysis, the P style also has some serious drawbacks. P's are often poor at time management, follow-up, and attention to detail. They exaggerate, appearing untrustworthy, especially to M's. The P usually has to work on managing time, sticking to the facts, and remembering to inject hard data into presentations.

THE S (SUPPORTIVE) STYLE: DEVELOPING CREDIBILITY THROUGH RELATIONSHIP BUILDING

In one company for which I consulted, there was a legendary salesperson named Wayne. If you were dealing with folks who had been customers, even as far back as 10 or 15 years, they would always ask, "How's Wayne?" They remembered Wayne, liked Wayne, often invited Wayne to their children's weddings. And these customers bought product from him like nobody's business. Wayne was an S.

S's sell or influence through the power of being personally liked. The S is a person who's concerned about other people and reflects that concern in his behavior. When you deal with an S, you believe that he's truly concerned about your wellbeing and you like that; his concern influences you. In the service businesses, S's go out of their way to help customers. They extend themselves. They get up early in the morning or work late at night to be helpful and to provide the best service. Over time, they become closely attached to the people with whom they do business and often grow to be considered part of the customer's family. Quite obviously, such attachments give the S an important advantage in the influence department.

But sometimes this concern for people can work to the S's disadvantage. Being too concerned about other's feelings can prevent the S from making quick, objective decisions. One S I know has the problem of wanting to agree with everyone. If you go into his office and state your opinion, he'll agree with you because he wants to make you happy. If another person comes in with a conflicting opinion, he'll agree with that person, too. If a third comes in with yet another idea, well, he's all for that one as well. When this happens, when S's are more concerned with winning popularity contest than taking a required stand, they can lose the respect of their fellow workers. As managers, S's can often be stymied in resolving tough personnel problems. Firing someone is difficult for any manager; for an S it can be a nightmare.

The C (Competitive) Style: Developing Credibility through Persistence and Confrontation

The final style is the C style. The C's formula for successful influence is persistence and insistence. They probe, surface, and confront all objections until the customer just caves in. C's are fond of asserting that the sale doesn't start until the customer says no.

C's enjoy conflict. If you don't stand up to them, if you aren't willing to disagree with them, they quickly lose respect for you. If there is no conflict, they sometimes go out of their way to create it. S's, on the other hand, seek harmony, prefer to avoid conflict, and are often inept at handling it. M's think conflict is a waste of time. After all, the facts should speak for themselves.

The C.E.O. of Kimberly Clark put into words what many C's feel. "Every morning I look in the mirror and ask how I can beat the hell out of P&G. And I want everyone one of my employees to do the same".

Some C's are off-the-chart competitors. Take Bill Gates, the Chairman of Microsoft. One story about him goes that after losing a chess game he knocked all the pieces off the board. I also once read a story about Elaine Garzarelli, the famous investment guru who reported that when she was young, her mother told her not to come home if she lost in a competitive activity.

If a person repeatedly talks about how nice guys finish last, that person is probably a C. If a person says they do not care if people like them as long as they are respected, they are probably a C. If a person insists you cannot make an omelet without breaking some eggs, that person is probably a C. If a person tells you business is like warfare and the goal is to take no prisoners, that person is probably a C. And if a person has a tattoo of Vince Lombardi, the Green Bay Packers coach, you can be sure that person is a C.

When I play tennis with a C, there is a gambit which I use to have fun and to make a little money. Before the match, I suggest we have a wager so there is money on the line. After we play a few games, I wait until my opponent hits a ball which is clearly out. I say: "Great shot!"

Since the C would never make a line call which gave his opponent the point, I have shaken the very foundation of the way he plays the game. The computer in his brain is knocked out from this literally mind-blowing event. Since the circuits in the brain have gone haywire, he can hardly walk, let alone play well. (By the time he recovers, I have won the match and collected the money.)

C's, when they are younger, attempt to get their way through some combination of assertion and intimidation. They are often perceived as ruthlessly ambitious. They can run roughshod over people. They can be too impulsive in making decisions and not sensitive enough to the feelings of others.

When these individuals develop insight into the disadvantages of their style and make some appropriate modifications, they become incredibly effective. When they don't change and their essential attitudes remain the same, they end up on one of the lists you see from time to time in business articles about the Ten Worst Bosses.

In clarifying this model of the four styles, it is often helps to use a template based on famous people and their styles.

Influence Styles of Famous People

The M Type

Personal Characteristics	Quiet, reserved, formal, fact-oriented, organized, independent, calm, unemotional
Probable M's	Jackie Onassis, Tiger Woods, Mahatma Ghandi

The P Type

Personal Characteristics	Enthusiastic, informal, animated in conversation, love the dramatic, need recognition, enjoy the limelight
Probable P's	Carol Burnett, Teddy Roosevelt, Robin Williams

The S Type

Personal Characteristics	Warm, friendly, outgoing, people-oriented, easily approachable, easy to talk to, avoid conflict
Probable S's	Julia Roberts, Bill Cosby, Mel Gibson

The C Type

Personal Characteristics	Domineering, forceful, competitive, task-oriented, enjoy conflict
Probable C's	Margaret Thatcher, Bill Gates, Madonna

When you begin designing an influence strategy for your next customer, start by figuring out whether they are like Mahatma Ghandi, Winston Churchill, Bill Cosby, or

Margaret Thatcher?

A simple way to apply the model is to think of all the people you know and identify the four who come closest to being the purest example of each of the four styles. When you meet a person for the first time, use your personal prototypes to help you determine your best approach.

HOW WOULD YOU SELL A BOAT TO DIFFERENT PEOPLE?

If you grasp the fundamental concepts, you should be able to understand how you would sell a person a specific product. We are going to use a boat for discussion purposes.

How would you sell a boat to an M? Well, if it were me, I'd start by giving the M the owner's manual, saying, "Here is a book of instructions about the boat, containing all the data on the boat that has ever been printed. I'm going to walk you through this manual and teach you everything about this boat." The M needs lots of information to make a decision; M's need to deal with issues in a rational manner. You need to give M's the comfort that they have enough data to deal effectively with this purchase.

With a P, I'd appeal to his or her sense of drama. I might say to a P: "Picture yourself in the outfit worn by the commodore of the yacht club. Picture the gold braids on your sleeve. Picture the brass buttons." P's need to receive recognition and attention. Your job is to convey how that need will be addressed through your product or idea.

Of course, you'd tell S's that they could invite all their friends onto the boat. You'd have them visualize the happy, harmonious group of people they'd take out onto the lake with them, all laughing and drinking margaritas as the sun sets. If you were selling an S an idea, you'd say that everyone else you've spoken with already agrees. You'd appeal to their need to be liked, and the next thing the S would say is, "Where do I sign?"

The way to sell a C a boat is almost painfully obvious. What would you say? "You are going to have the fastest boat on the lake." You also need to be somewhat confrontational with C's, as well as persistent and insistent to mirror their styles.

WHAT TO DO WHEN THE STYLE IS NOT OBVIOUS

It can sometimes be difficult to figure another person out. Maybe it's difficult to observe that person closely enough to determine his or her style. Maybe this person uses a mix of styles or is simply hard to interpret. Maybe you don't know them well. In these cases, here are a few pointers.

Try the direct approach. Ask the individual what you need to do differently in order to work effectively with them. Sometimes that works amazingly well, yet sometimes it's a waste of time.

Use the indirect approach. Ask someone who has an excellent relationship with the person in question and find out the best way to influence or communicate with them.

Finally, if these strategies both fail, experiment. You may get lucky and stumble on the right approach. I have witnessed many situations when, out of desperation, the person who had failed to influence "the customer" tried something radically different and was successful.

A number of years ago I was consulting with a firm whose vice president of sales did not believe in pampering people, and he was against the idea of spending extra money to equip sales representatives' cars with air conditioning this was when air conditioning was an option, not standard equipment. All arguments people used with him fell on deaf ears. However, in Dayton, Ohio, there was a very clever representative who had a talent for thinking out of the box. One year, during August, when the temperature was breaking all records, the vice president was scheduled to fly into Dayton to meet with some important customers. His plane was due at 4 PM. The sales representative drove his car to the airport at 8 AM and parked it in the parking lot, making very sure that all the windows and vents were closed. He took a cab back to his office, and had the cab pick him up in the afternoon, in time for him to meet the vice president's plane. You can imagine what happened. When the two men came out to get in the car, the temperature in the car must have been over 100°. The vice president was soaked with perspiration within two minutes. Later that day, after his meeting, he called his assistant back at the home office and left instructions that air conditioners should be installed in all cars, as soon as possible.

When you're trying to influence someone, think of yourself as a sports car with four forward speeds. Just as you would shift the gears in this car when you encountered different driving conditions, you need to shift your influence style depending on your customer.

That said, I don't suggest that you become an influence chameleon. While flexibility is important, so is being yourself being genuine. Build on your strengths. If you are a P, be the best darn P you can be. Also minimize your weaknesses. Become more aware of the shortcomings of your style so you can decrease the number of times it gets you into trouble. You've heard this before, but it's true: in influence, as in the rest of life, it takes all kinds.

WHAT'S YOUR INFLUENCE STYLE?

This model can be used to help you get more insight into yourself. What is your style? Does your self-analysis coincide with the way other people see you?

Here is a simple diagnostic instrument. Say you had four options for activities to pursue after reading this chapter:

1. Go out and deal with a disgruntled customer, someone other people have not been able to sell, or someone who does not particularly like your company.

2. Attend a meeting of the United Way, as an ambassador of good will representing your company.

3. Analyze a stack of data, work alone, and prepare a report for your immediate supervisor.

4. Give a lecture to 200 people.

Which of these activities would you choose to do? Don't choose the one that you think you would do best. Pick the one that you would enjoy doing, the one that would give you the greatest amount of psychic income. Put them in rank order.

Based on your choice, your primary influence style is likely to be the following:

1. Disgruntled customer: Style C. If you like to engage in controversy or conflict, win over someone who's a tough customer, be successful where others have failed, you clearly like to operate in the C style.

2. Goodwill ambassador: Style S. If you most look forward to the opportunity to meet new people, make friends, and get them to feel good, you are probably primarily an S.

3. Data analysis: Style M. If you like to deal with information and like to work fairly independently, without a lot of other people around, you probably prefer the M style.

4. Lecture an audience: Style P. If you relish an audience and love a chance to perform, you are most likely a P. I once gave these choices to a group in a lecture. One participant (evidently missing the theoretical nature of the question) was so excited about the opportunity to talk to a captive audience, he actually ran right out of the room to find an auditorium. A prototypical P!

Because each of these styles has definite and unique advantages and disadvantages, it's essential that you know your primary style, so you can effectively build on the advantages and work on mitigating the disadvantages.

FLEXIBILITY IS THE KEY

At this point, you may be wishing I was here in person so you could argue with me personally. Ed, you might say, I don't fit neatly into any one of these little boxes. I have a lot of C in me, but I'm also a bit of a P. Or, I can't choose between M and S; I feel evenly divided between both. Or even better, I'm sure I have a primary style, but I find I can be a P, S, M, or C effectively, depending on whom I'm dealing with.

Congratulations! You're already on your way to the next step in improving your ability to influence people: learning to be flexible in your style based on the mode of your target, or the person you're trying to influence.

Notice that throughout this discussion I've referred to your primary pattern of influence. While some of us may truly be ambidextrous in using the four styles, most of us do have one primary mode in which we most comfortably operate. On the other hand, almost all of us have the ability to work in more than one style adequately.

Capitalizing on this flexibility is the key to improving your influence capability. In any industry, at any point in time, if you obtained a list of the top 10 sales representatives, you can predict with a high level of certainty that you will find a mixture of M's, S's, C's, and P's. This is a clear demonstration of the fact that there is no one single best style.

These successful sales people are more flexible. They make choices based on the style of the customer.

If you're an M, I can make the choice not to kid around with you too much because you're probably a serious type of person. (If you had known Jackie Kennedy when she was alive, you probably wouldn't have slapped her on the back and told off-color stories.) I can choose to avoid exaggerating (which a P would easily accept) and stick with the facts.

If you're an S, I can choose to work to convert you to being a friend of mine. I can be conscious of the high value you place on keeping people happy. If you are a P, I can generate excitement. If you are C, I can ally myself with your desire to beat the competition.

We all have a fairly wide behavioral repertoire, and we can use this flexibility to our advantage.

PREDICTING BEHAVIOR

We have been talking about doing a better job of influencing through using the model. It can also be very helpful in improving your ability to predict behavior.

Next week, I could go into any company and give a vivid demonstration of how this model can be used to predict behavior. I would explain the basic concept to a large group and then ask for seven volunteers representing each of the four styles. I would ask the participants to divide into groups in separate rooms and would give them a team assignment. Although you have spent maybe fifteen minutes reading this material, if I told you to observe each group for maybe ten minutes each, you would be able with little difficulty to identify each group. The P's are all talking, waving their hands. They're telling jokes, having a good time. Almost never is only one person speaking at once. That's against the P's rule; they all want to be at the center of the stage.

In the S room, you'd have to come near the group to hear them. They are more soft-spoken, frighteningly polite. One S says, "Why don't you go first?" The second S says, "No, please take your turn." you first. They are so nice to each other, so pleasant. They are appallingly agreeable.

What would you expect in the M room? That's right, flip charts. Not only that, but flip charts with their ideas organized into 1, 1A, 1B, 2, 2A, 2B, etc. The M group is very quiet, very reserved, and very, very professional.

With the C's, though, it's another story. If you walked into their room you would likely find yourself in the middle of a big power struggle, as the group decides who is going to be the leader. When I give groups like these a task, they often don't complete it, because of all the infighting.

POINTS TO REMEMBER

The mind is like a submarine with water tight compartments. Although, we know for certain people are different, we frequently treat them as if they were just like us. The model presented in this chapter is not the be all end all. However, it can help you to pin point how some people are very much like you and some are quite different.

Utilizing Feedback to Make Course Corrections

When Benjamin Franklin was a young man, an older friend of his took him aside and said something like this:

"Ben, you are impossible. Your opinions have a slap in them for anyone who differs with you. Your friends find they enjoy themselves better when you are not around. You know so much that no man can tell you anything; indeed, no man is going to try."

Franklin took this advice to heart. He worked hard to change the way he dealt with people and, as everyone knows, grew up to become a statesman and a diplomat, as well as an author and inventor.

In his autobiography, Tom Watson, the son of the founder of IBM, tells how he never accomplished much in either high school or college, and how he didn't find any thing that suited his talents until he became a pilot in World War II.

In his book, *Like Father, Like Son*, he relates the following story.

> "In the spring of 1945, I was back in Washington D.C. and asked General Bradley (the general who had commanded Watson's outfit) to come have dinner with Olive and me. Our conversation…is riveted in my mind, because it completely changed my life.
>
> He said, "Tom, what are you going to do when the war is over?"
>
> "Well, General, I've got a job lined up that I think I'm going to take. I'm going to be a pilot with United Air Lines."
>
> He said. "Really, I always thought you'd go back and run the IBM Company".
>
> I was stunned. "General Bradley", I said, "Do you think I could run IBM?" And he said, "Of course."

After dinner, Watson talked it over with his wife, who felt he could do anything he set his mind to, and 24 hours later, he called his father to ask if he could come to work for IBM.

Franklin, the brash know-it-all, didn't have a clue that the way he treated people was not in his best interests. Watson had no idea of how highly he was regarded by a man whose opinion he held in high regard. Both of these are dramatic examples of how feedback—either positive or negative—can change the course of a person's life. Not many people get feedback that has such dramatic results, but these two examples clearly illustrate why utilizing feed-back to make course corrections is one of the three crucial interpersonal competencies.

In this chapter, we will discuss:

- The basics of feedback

- Types of feedback

- Land mines and obstacles

- Eight suggestions

THE BASICS OF FEEDBACK

When I think of feedback, five thoughts come to mind.

1. As I work with people, I inevitably create both positive and negative reactions. It's helpful to know the positive reactions, but they can't hurt me. It much more helpful to know the negative reactions because, if I am not aware of them, they can hurt me to one degree or another.

2. I have never gotten up in the morning and made a promise to myself that I was going to make a mistake. I have never planned to offend anyone. I have never deliberately set out to frighten anyone. I have never planned to confuse people. Yet, I have done all of the above. You and I do not consciously or deliberately make mistakes. We do not make mistakes on purpose. We make them unconsciously.

When we make mistakes, how can we become aware of them unless someone tells us? Feedback is not just helpful, it is essential.

3. I am always conscious of what people might be saying behind my back. Talking about people behind their backs is a national pastime. We all do it. What happens, for example, when a group of individuals who have worked together for several years get a new leader? A massive effort takes place as people compare notes and the new leader quickly starts to get a reputation. Does the new leader find out about the assessments that are being made of him or her?

In training sessions, we can sometimes replicate what occurs naturally. Imagine fifteen people in a room seated at a U-shaped table. They all know each other. I'll ask one person to sit in a chair at the open end of the table, with the back of the chair turned toward the group. I say, "We've all said things about so-and-so behind his back, right? I want you to tell him right now some of the things you have said behind his back." The person in the chair is instructed to remain silent and to avoid making a rebuttal.

It amazes me how effective this simulation can be. In many cases, people do open up and say things they would never have thought of saying to the other person's face, things that can be helpful to the recipient. And it is astonishing what people can learn about themselves in these training sessions.

Wouldn't you like to know what people say behind your back? Could that help you? What about the risk of not knowing what people are saying?

4. When I was in the Army, I was on the rifle team. After I shot several rounds at a target, a person in a bunker down range would hold up a marker that covered the bullet holes. This would show if my shot was high, low, off to the left, or off to the right. Once I knew the direction and magnitude of the error, I could experiment with different modifications until I found the right one. Maybe I just needed to adjust the sight. Maybe I flinched when I pulled the trigger, making the shot go high. Maybe I was not holding the weapon properly. How could I have improved my marks-

manship without feedback? How can *you* become more effective without it?

The marksman has a goal: hitting the bull's-eye more often and improving the score. At given points in time, you also are trying to achieve certain goals, such as getting a budget approved, selling an innovative idea, or trying to get a subordinate promoted. The parallel with the marksman analogy is that you need feedback to help you achieve your goals.

This analogy is somewhat flawed because, when you are learning to improve your marksmanship, all feedback is valuable and should never be ignored. When it comes to interpersonal feedback, some feedback should be ignored. Examples are given in the next section.

5. Finally, I am always cognizant of the fact that small changes in behavior can lead to the difference between success and failure. We all know some people know how to tell jokes and some don't. One person can get everyone laughing loudly while the same joke, when told by an amateur, goes over like a lead balloon. The differences in the two presentations are slight—a difference in timing, emphasis, tone of voice or body language—but the differences in outcome are dramatic. There are numerous examples in professional tennis of players who win their first major tournament only after getting a new coach who helps them to make small changes in their game. In baseball, batting .300 versus .250 is a matter of getting one more hit every twenty times at bat. Do you think the game of business is different from professional sports?

TYPES OF FEEDBACK

Let's start by talking about two types of feedback which are usually not helpful. Some feedback reveals more about the sender than the recipient. In other instances, you get contradictory messages.

Too often, feedback tells us more about the sender than the receiver. This is often the case in performance reviews. In too many cases, the implicit message the reviewer gives to his or her subordinates is simply that "You need to be more like me." In other words, the nitpicker tells his subordinates to pay more attention to detail; the charismatic leader instructs his followers to be more enthusiastic; the take-no-prisoners executive exhorts his underlings to be more tough-minded. In these cases, the person giving the feedback has come to the conclusion that their way is the right way and that you would benefit if you were more like them.

Feedback that is contradictory is not helpful. Some people say that you are not aggressive enough and others insist you are too aggressive. In most cases like this, you have to let your intuition and experience be your guide. Maybe you are too pushy with certain kinds of people and need to be aware of that.

Useful feedback can be categorized as either simple or complex. Simple feedback contains a prescription for change, while complex feedback does not. When you are given simple feedback, the message is to do more or less or stop doing it. For example, some individuals are told they should talk less and listen more. Granted, it may be difficult for them to discipline themselves, but the feedback is crystal clear.

There are other instances in which the receiver needs to stop doing something. When I started giving lectures, I got feedback that I would often look up at the ceiling which distracted the audience. I worked hard to correct the habit. From then on, I was very conscious of the importance of eye contact with the audience. When I gave a lecture to a new group, I would make it a point to take the initiative and ask them if I was distracting them. In some cases, before the lecture, I would ask someone to observe me and tell me if I was doing better. I gradually improved.

This example illustrates that it takes time, effort, and monitoring to make changes. Second, it shows that I was motivated to change because I was doing something that was not in my best interest. Third, once my problem was identified, I was able to ask people ahead of time, instead of retrospectively, to observe and critique my performance. Getting feedback is an ongoing process. You act, get input, and make appropriate course corrections. Then, you need to get more feedback to see if the corrective steps you took had a demonstrable effect. Sometimes you ask open-ended questions like: "What can I do better?" At other times, you focus on specifics like: "Did I talk too much?"

While simple feedback contains a clear blueprint for change, complex feedback presents you with a puzzle to be solved. Examples of complex feedback can include:

"You are immature."

"You are not a good leader."

"You do not handle conflict well."

Obviously, in these cases, you need to probe, get clarification, and ask for examples or specific ideas of what you can do differently. In sorting out such issues, identifying a role model is helpful. For example, if you have the reputation of being immature, you should try to identify someone in your age group who has a reputation for being very mature, analyze the differences and learn from those lessons. Also, remember in the rifle example, the feedback gave a fix on the kind of error (the bullets were hitting the target to the left of the bull's-eye) but did not tell what corrective action to take. In the art of marksmanship and interpersonal feedback you often need to experiment to zero in on the bull's-eye.

Feedback can be positive or negative. When you are criticized, you must quickly decide what to do, because the two avenues available to you are totally different. On the one hand, let us say you are criticized unfairly and it is imperative to set the record straight immediately. The need to set the record straight becomes your number one priority and you should vigorously defend yourself. However, if your prime priority is to learn, then you take an opposite tack; you must be non-defensive, listen, and pay attention.

I have emphasized the importance of soliciting negative feedback. When you create positive reactions, you can't be hurt. However, when people react to you in a negative way, you can be hurt. I do not want to de-emphasize the value of positive feedback. Positive feedback can make you feel good, reinforce the good things you do, give you reassurance that you are on the right track, and make you more confident.

LAND MINES AND OBSTACLES

I believe that getting helpful feedback can be as difficult as it is essential. There are hurdles which need to be overcome. In many instances, this results from hierarchical relationships.

What are the barriers to giving feedback to people higher in the chain of command? Fear of retaliation is probably the most frequent one. There is a dramatic example of the influence of fear, which I will never forget. In preparing for an offsite team building meeting for the direct reports of a Vice President of Operations in a large manufacturing facility in West Point, Pennsylvania, I met with each of the key people before the meeting. We reviewed the purpose, objectives and ground rules. I explained to one of them, whom I knew fairly well, that one part of the meeting would focus on individual feedback.

He frowned when I mentioned that, because he knew his peers would not feel comfortable giving feedback to the Vice President. He looked at me and said, "Ed, if you really think this exercise will be beneficial, I will go along with you. But, when I give Charlie (the boss) feedback, I want a photo of my wife and kids, a copy of my mortgage, and the certificate honoring me for twenty-five years of service with the company right behind me!" I managed to find a credible excuse for canceling the training session. When the level of fear is high, the quality of feedback disintegrates. Consequently, there was little value in conducting a teambuilding session.

What problems occur in giving feedback from top down in the chain of command?

The largest barrier that inhibits the free flow of feedback has to do with the generally accepted management rule that it is better to give criticism in private and praise in public. Let's say you make a presentation to a group of people that includes many people more senior in authority. Following the rule, they would not give you negative feedback because they want to avoid embarrassing you in public. Also, they don't give you feedback because they are rushing to another meeting. So, you may never get feedback that could have helped you.

There are also line/staff barriers. Line people can't be successful in resolving certain issues unless they get the cooperation of the staff. The odds are that the line managers are not going to offer feedback. Why? They need the help of the staff person and they don't want to take the risk of jeopardizing their relationship. In their judgment, they have more to lose than to gain. And, most importantly, they don't see it as part of their job.

These barriers can be overcome by having an executive coach or by getting 360° feedback, a formal process for getting input from many different sources. The person who truly understands the importance of feedback realizes it's his or her responsibility to get it. He or she proactively seeks feedback and benefits from it.

EIGHT SUGGESTIONS

1. Everyone needs a Willy or a Wilhelmina, someone who works closely with you, is basically on your side, and can be counted on to give you candid feedback. When Jack Kennedy was selecting his cabinet, Joe Kennedy, his father, insisted that Bobby Kennedy, who was totally unqualified for the job, be made Attorney General of the United States. The senior Kennedy believed that Jack had to have someone who would give him the unvarnished truth, someone he could trust completely.

2. Take the initiative. One of the primary reasons you need to seek feedback, rather than wait for it, is that people can be reluctant to volunteer criticism. If you don't ask them and are insincere about wanting to know, they will never tell you. It is necessary to flush the birds out of the bushes. Make it easier for people to give you feedback by asking for it directly.

3. Learning to ask the right kind of questions in getting feedback is somewhat of an art form. Essentially, you always have to be aware that, for a variety of reasons, someone might be inhibited and not be totally forthcoming. A great question for increasing the chances of getting the straight story is to say to a person, "Don't tell me what you think. Tell me what others think."

4. When you get feedback and your objective is to learn, you must listen and not become defensive. When faced with criticism, it is natural to question its validity and want to argue the points. To protect your self-esteem, you may want to explain to the conveyers of feedback why they don't understand the situation, why it's someone else's fault, and why you have some excuse for not doing better. When you ask for feedback, however, you've got to resist all these human tendencies in order to keep the channels of communication open.

5. Receiving feedback often requires patience. Many times people will start by mentioning rather innocuous comments before getting to the heart of the matter. Once I conducted a weeklong training program in a resort area. It happened that I returned home on the same plane as the vice president of marketing, the highest-level participant. Naturally, I asked him for feedback. The first criticism he had was one I believed was unfair, unsubstantiated, and incorrect. Though I was tempted to punch him in the mouth, I instead asked him to continue. The fourth piece of negative feedback he gave me ultimately turned out to be incredibly helpful. The feedback process is fragile and is easy to derail, and must be approached with diligence and patience for optimal results. You will be more successful if you realize that when people give you feedback they are inclined to give you the easy stuff first. Only if you respond appropriately will they reveal the criticisms of a more serious nature. So, you need to be patient, listen and, by all means, avoid being defensive.

6. Each time you change jobs and get a new manager, you have a prime opportunity to get feedback. At the right moment, you say something of this nature to your new boss "I know you have talked to several people about me. I also know, from my own experience, in almost 100% of job moves, people have reservations about the person they promote. It would be enormously helpful if you told me your reservations."

Suppose you had done this each time you got a new boss. I am sure two things would have happened. In some cases, you would have learned nothing. The response would have been that the only significant reservation had to do with, for example, your inexperience. In other cases, you would have learned valuable lessons. When you get feedback, you never know what you may unearth. For this reason, you must to take advantage of every opportunity that presents itself.

7. Be wary of apple polishers. From the first moment a person is put into a supervisory job, he or she begins to realize that a certain percentage of subordinates will do or say things only because they feel it's the politically wise thing to do. So, these people will tell you that you're perfect, you have the Wisdom of Solomon, and you're the best manager they've ever had. Should you believe them?

8. Finally, and most importantly, focus on getting the biggest bang for the buck. Assume a person is effective 80% of the time in the way they go about achieving their goals. However, 20% of the time, their approach is counterproductive. Within this 20%, 10% represents opportunities for improvement. The secret for most people is to set a priority to focus on the *one aspect* of how they interact with people that: *(1) can be changed, and (2) will have the biggest positive impact on their ability to achieve their personal goals.*

The remaining 10% has to do with traits that cannot or should not be modified. For example, some individuals love to dig into detail, often discovering critical information overlooked by others. It is one of their strengths. (Even though they may get feedback about being a micromanager, they are not likely to change.)

POINTS TO REMEMBER

I have never planned to offend anyone. I have never deliberately set out to frighten anyone. I have never confused people on purpose. Yet, I have done all of the above. You and I do not consciously or deliberately make mistakes. We do not make mistakes on purpose. *We make them unconsciously.* Unconscious incompetence is inevitable. The only known antidote is getting feedback that can be used to make course corrections. This type of feedback is as rare as it is valuable.

Section 3

Attributes and Attitudes

A Psychological Profile of People with Common Sense

Common Sense and Ego-Strength

Common sense is the ability to read a situation and to respond appropriately. The issues change as do the individuals involved. However, *you are the one constant in all situations*. And, of course, we all make independent decisions—others are not involved—and we have made mistakes for a variety of reasons. For example, we have been superficial rather than thorough in our analysis, or we became too emotional, or we were guilty of fire/ready/aim. As Pogo said, "We have met the enemy and he is us."

The question, is: what are the distinguishing characteristics of individuals who show a high degree of common sense? What sets them apart? I have concluded, after much reflection, that these people have high ego-strength. Ego-strength is multifaceted and complex. Below is a short list of the observable characteristics of these individuals. They listen, understand the view points of others, and are willing to change their position. Also, they are:

• Self-assured/confident, comfortable with themselves

• Realistic optimists

• Levelheaded

• Genuine

• Flexible

There are other qualities which cannot be directly observed. The best-in-breed can truthfully say they match up to the standard set by the author of Zorba The Greek who wrote his own epitaph:

I hate no one.
I fear no one.
I envy no one.
I am free.

The following is a more in-depth profile of people who have high ego-strength.

THEY ARE NOT STAMPEDED BY THE HERD

A critical characteristic of people with high self-esteem is that they are independent thinkers. When the herd stampedes, they don't necessarily follow because group pressures have little effect on them. We all have to make these kinds of choices about whether to go along with the crowd, adopt a neutral position, or go in a different direction.

Two psychological experiments tested the effect of group pressure and uncovered this hidden attribute of the individual with high self-esteem. In the first, psychology students at Columbia University in New York conducted a classic study on the power of peer pressure. In this study, a lookout person posted on a hill in Central Park would watch for a lone person strolling toward a specific point on the path. At the lookout's signal, another researcher would begin to fake an epileptic attack, directly in the path of the oncoming subject. Between 80 and 85 percent of these lone subjects would rush to comfort the "victim," trying to be helpful.

In the second part of the study, the lookout would again watch for a lone pedestrian, but at the signal, the lone stroller would be joined by a group of five other researchers, pretending to accidentally be walking the same route. As the group reached the same point on the path, another researcher would again begin faking an epileptic attack. The five researchers were instructed to resist assisting the fake seizure victim. In this case, only about 10 percent of the lone subjects would resist the peer pressure and go to the aid of the apparent victim.

The conclusion is clear: left to their own devices, most people will do the right thing. When there is group pressure, most people will not necessarily do the right thing. Only those with confidence in their own judgment will ignore the herd. (This study was done before the impact of trial lawyers with respect to helping people in distress. Some percentages might change because of their impact, but the conclusions of the research are the same.)

For the second example, imagine that when you were in college, someone had conned you into participating in a psychological study on perception. The purpose of the study, of which you were unaware, was to explore the power of group pressure.

You are ushered into a room with 12 other students and are asked to sit around a U-shaped table. Your name card is No. 12. The instructor then shows some slides of drawings. One slide might have five geometrical shapes, and the members of the group are asked to identify the two that are the most similar. The instructor questions each student, in turn, starting with the individual in the number one chair, then number 2, and so on, until he gets around to you, number 12. In each case, you have heard the answers of the other 11 participants before you are required to respond.

Things proceed very smoothly. The first several questions are easy. In each case, all 12 people give the same answer and you are quite relaxed. What you have not been told is that the other 11 people are "plants" confederates of the researcher. They have been told exactly what to say when the next slide appears.

Now the instructor shows a slide with four vertical lines, labeled a, b, c, and x. It looks like this:

The Perception Test

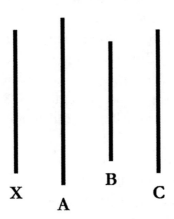

You look at it and it is very obvious to you that C is the correct answer. However, student number one picks B, as does 2, and so forth. In the end, all 11 students have chosen B.

At this point, most individuals conclude that there must be something wrong with them (perhaps they need new glasses). They decide the majority must be right. Even though line C looks the most like line X to them, they tell the instructor that B is the correct answer.

Only a minority—the ones with high ego-strength stick to their guns. They didn't conform. They stuck to their original conclusion, even when 11 others said the answer was B.

THEY ARE NOT INTIMIDATED BY AUTHORITY FIGURES

Not only do individuals with high self-esteem assert their independence and resist group pressure, they also resist the pressure most of us feel to comply with authority figures.

A number of years ago at Texas A&M, a famous mathematics instructor taught a course in advanced calculus. At the end of one semester, he gave a take-home quiz. The class was given twenty equations to solve before they came to the next lecture.

The instructor called on one student to write the solution to the first problem a long, involved equation on the blackboard. The student had barely begun when the professor said, "No, that's wrong. Sit down." He called on another, who came up and started writing. This student was also was told that he wrong and was sent back to his seat. The professor called on a third student with the same outcome. Then a fourth student was called to the board. He was interrupted as the others were and told to sit down. When, like the other students, he was told to sit down because he was wrong, he looked the professor right in the eye and said, "No, professor, I am right. You are wrong."

The professor then turned to the class and said, "You see, it isn't enough to be right. You have to (have the confidence to) know you are right."

If the pressure of groups or authority figures fails to make a dent in the courage of your convictions, then you are home free.

THEY ACCEPT THEIR GENETICALLY FIXED ADVANTAGES AND DISADVANTAGES

When you do an in depth analysis of people who are free from the internal pressure to conform to groupthink and who are not intimidated by authority figures, you will find that their level of self-acceptance is high. These individuals "accept the things about themselves they cannot change, have the courage to change they things they can, and have the wisdom to know the difference," paraphrasing a quote from Reinhold Niebuhr, the famous theologian.

There are certain things about ourselves we cannot change. These traits are rooted in our genes. They are part of our DNA. We need to accept them.

Some of these fixed characteristics can affect our self-esteem depending on how others evaluate them. For example, our society places a premium on athletic prowess. People who are physically attractive are put on a pedestal. Individuals of high intelligence are held in high esteem.

There is no question that these traits are genetically determined. If you are very talented, incredibly attractive, and intellectually gifted, you are blessed. However, most of us fall short in one or more of these categories. Where would you place in a talent show? Although beauty is in the eye of the beholder, how would you rank in your company if someone held a contest? How would you measure on intelligence tests compared to your coworkers?

The answer is the same for all of us on these and similar questions: On any scale there are, and always will be, people above you and people below you. Learning to live with that is what we call self-acceptance. People with a high degree of self-acceptance don't argue with reality. They don't undervalue themselves because they can't win the beauty contest. Conversely, they don't become egotistical and overbearing because they're bright; they know that there will always be someone brighter. What they have is a balanced perspective.

Those individuals with low esteem have trouble playing the hand they were dealt. They're bothered by being too thin or too fat, too tall or too short; the list of inadequacies is endless.

Clearly, self-acceptance is not just a matter of genetics. For example, I have known at least 100 executives who never graduated from college, usually because they hadn't been able to afford it. Some of them never think twice about it; they don't feel inferior when they walk into a room of more highly educated colleagues. On the other hand, some do brood and go through life with a nagging feeling that they will never be as worthwhile as their college-degreed peers.

Along these lines, I've always been fond of a story about Eisenhower. It illustrates how cleverness or ingenuity is often a prerequisite to feeling good about yourself. After the war, Eisenhower became the President of Columbia University. At his inaugural ceremony, he had to give a talk to the faculty. He felt somewhat overpowered by the presence of so many scholars, so many people with multiple advanced degrees. How did he keep his composure? According to his memoirs, he imagined they were all in their underwear. (Eisenhower, who you would think was one of the most confident of all people, had to resort to mental gymnastics to bolster his confidence. We will discuss these kinds of tricks in more depth later on.)

THEY DON'T PUT THEMSELVES OR OTHERS DOWN

People who accept themselves do not put themselves down. They believe Eleanor Roosevelt was right when she said, "No one can make me feel inferior but myself."

You are in a team meeting and someone says, "I have an idea, but you probably won't like it," or "You'll probably think what I'm going to say is stupid." I hear people denigrate themselves and sell themselves short all the time. These individuals have such low self-esteem, they have to put themselves down before someone else does.

Sometimes we put ourselves down more subtly in our reaction to honest praise. We'll blush, deny, or say, "You're being too kind." We have difficulty accepting compliments, feeling unworthy. If you fit the description of any of the above, you clearly suffer from some degree of low self-esteem.

Conversely, people with high self-esteem do not put others down. Individuals who put others down are trying to feel better about themselves. It never works. Put-downs come in a variety of flavors.

"You went to college at Illinois—Normal? I went to Smith."

"You have a swimming pool, boat, car, or house? Mine is bigger, better, and costs more money."

"Oh, you're engaged? What a sweet little ring!"

When I began consulting, I worked with people in an engineering firm. It was their steadfast conviction that there were two kinds of people in the world: (1) the first class people who were fortunate enough to have been trained as engineers, and (2) everyone else. In other words, you didn't count if you hadn't gone to engineering school. You were second class.

Then there's Lady Astor, who reportedly told Sir Winston Churchill that if he were her husband, she would poison him. He replied that if he was married to her, he would drink the poison.

Indeed, the things for which we put others down can be really quite amazing. I have some friends who moved to a swank area in California and went to a cocktail party to meet their neighbors. They learned that, in this town, you are what you drive. If you drove a Rolls Royce, you'd be surrounded by people wanting to be your friends. If you had a Mercedes, you might still make some friends. But God help the couple who confessed to driving a Toyota! People shunned them as though they were lepers.

THEY AVOID SHOOTING THEMSELVES IN THE FOOT

People who accept themselves have a realistic and clear idea of their shortcomings. We all have an Achilles heel—a trait or predisposition that can get us into trouble. Maybe it is impatience, indecisiveness, or an inability to handle conflict or to accept criticism from superiors. Many of us have a problem with losing our temper. The trick is to develop some mechanism which enables us to prevent our shortcoming from getting us in serious difficulty.

A good example involves Dwight Eisenhower. He recognized that he had a short fuse and, when his temper got out of control, he was prone to do or say things he would later regret. He realized he had to do something about it. When he got mad, he wrote the offending person a letter and put it in the lower left-hand drawer of his desk for ten days. When the time was up, he reviewed the letter and sent it only if it still reflected how he felt. Eisenhower only sent about 10 or 15 percent of the letters he wrote. Writing them allowed him catharsis without causing irreparable damage.

In essence, he had a clear idea of his fatal flaw and created an ingenious remedy. What's your fatal flaw? What is your remedy?

THEY MAKE THE RIGHT CAREER CHOICES

Self-acceptance and a realistic evaluation of ones strengths and weaknesses has many positive consequences. One of these is that the person is more likely to make good career choices.

Ron Gelbman had a spectacular career when he worked at Johnson & Johnson. Before he retired, he was responsible for a huge chunk of the company's profits. Earlier in his career, he ran a division which was badly in need of new products. Ron was able to license a product from Chiron, a biotech company. In the course of the negotiations, the cofounders developed a high regard for Ron. They ultimately offered him a job as the President.

They made him a very attractive offer. Ron knew himself very well: he was keenly aware that he was at his best when given a great deal of autonomy. As he examined the situation closely, he realized that, in all probability, the cofounders would not be able to give him the freedom he required. Therefore, he turned down the offer.

There are many other examples of individuals who have made great career choices because they were realistic in their self appraisal. Bill Gates went to Harvard with the idea of becoming a mathematician. He quickly found there were many members of his class who were more talented. He could not compete and excel in such a group, so he changed majors and embarked on a computer-based career. Alan Greenspan, the current Chairman of the Federal Reserve, started out to be a musician and quickly learned he did not have the right stuff to be one of the best, so he decided to attend college and set his sights on becoming an economist.

THEY LEARN TO TRUST THEIR INTUITION

Individuals who accept themselves and have high ego-strength learn to trust their intuition. Intuition comes in two flavors: one having everything to do with experience and the other type having nothing to do with experience.

In some situations when people talk about trusting their "instincts" or "having a gut feel," they really are tapping into what they have learned from experience. This leads them to some conclusion which is hard to articulate, or not easily justified without hard facts.

In other cases, choices are determined by something innate, unlearned, and not related to experience. When my daughter, Jenna, was 6-years-old I decided to teach her how to play backgammon. I explained the goal of the game and how it was played, but I didn't mention anything about strategy. As we started to play, I was amazed because she played as if she had read all the books on strategy. Depending on the position of all the pieces, she would make the moves which gave her the greatest advantage. She intuitively sensed what to do.

A story about Mozart is one of many about the role of intuition and the creative process. One day a man approached Mozart and asked him how to go about writing a symphony. He was told to start by writing a sonata. The man was insulted. He wanted to know why he had to start with sonatas while Mozart wrote his first symphony when he was 11-years-old. Mozart explained that, in his case, he didn't have to ask anyone how to write a symphony.

I believe if Mozart had tried to explain how he went about writing a symphony, it would have been difficult, if not impossible for him to do. This often happens in business. People who have good instincts have trouble articulating the reasons for reaching a conclusion and, as a result, may be ridiculed or ignored and ultimately fail to convince people that their idea was sound.

Growing Up Can Endanger Your Mental Health

Attaining a high level of emotional health is not easy. Many of us had experiences when we were young that now have a profound impact on our adult lives. When I was in grade school, I hated to go to a woodworking class on Wednesday afternoon. I couldn't saw a board straight. The nails would conspire against me, refusing to go in without bending. I never attained the skill required to do a proper job of using a plane to shape a piece of wood. Oh, how I dreaded Wednesdays.

In high school, it was gym class that defeated me. I couldn't run as fast, jump as high, or shoot baskets as well as the other kids in my class. It didn't make me feel good about myself. And in college I had to work at the stockyards to earn money. The pay was good and I liked being out in the fresh air, but after twelve hours of exposure to the smell of stockyards, no one would sit next to me on the bus. Believe me, I had an inferiority complex in the making!

The following fable illustrates how education can be dangerous to your emotional health, how people emerge from the school with some strong negative feelings about themselves.

Fable for School People
By G.H. Reavis
Assistant Superintendent, Cincinnati Public Schools
"Once upon a time, the animals decided they must do something heroic to meet the problems of 'a new world.' So they organized a school.

They adopted an activity curriculum consisting of running, climbing, swimming, and flying. To make it easier to administer the curriculum, all the animals took all the subjects.

The duck was excellent in swimming, in fact better than his instructor; but he made only passing grades in flying and was very poor in running. Since he was slow in running, he had to stay after school and also drop swimming in order to practice running. This was kept up until his web feet were badly worn and he was only average in swimming. But average was acceptable in school, so nobody worried about that except the duck.

The rabbit started at the top of the class in running, but had a nervous breakdown because of so much makeup work in swimming.

The squirrel was excellent in climbing until he developed frustration in the flying class, where his teacher made him start from the ground up instead of from the treetop down. He also developed a 'charley horse' from overexertion and got a C in climbing and a D in running.

The eagle was a problem child and was disciplined severely. In climbing class he beat all the others to the top of the tree, but insisted on using his own way to get there.

At the end of the year, an abnormal eel that could swim exceedingly well, and also run, climb, and fly a little had the higher average and was valedictorian.

The prairie dogs stayed out of school and fought the tax levy because the administration would not add digging and burrowing to the curriculum. They apprenticed their children to a badger and later joined the groundhogs and gophers to start a successful private school."

Suppose you were the eagle. You should have been rewarded in school for excellence for being a better flyer than most of your classmates. Instead, you were punished because you were not good at climbing!

Maybe your negative feelings about yourself did not come from school. Maybe you were sure your mother or father loved one of your brothers or sisters much more than they loved you. I had a friend who was a really good student, but her brother was brilliant. She was very attractive, but, as she put it, no Venus de Milo. She had a good career as a business editor, but her friends were out there working as doctors, lawyers, and high-powered advertising executives. Though bright, beautiful and talented, she went through life feeling that somehow she just didn't measure up.

THEY USE PSYCHOLOGICAL CRUTCHES

You will recall the story about Eisenhower imagining the faculty of Columbia University dressed in their underwear. I have found that most people who achieve a high level of self-esteem need to engage in what can be called mental gymnastics or psychological crutches.

Squibb was one of the first American companies to enter the pharmaceutical business. I consulted with them before they were bought out by Bristol-Myers to form what is now known as Bristol-Myers Squibb. One day I was on the 12th floor of the Squibb building in Manhattan, the executive floor. Imagine how you would construct the set if you were filming a movie in an old fashioned executive suite with wood paneling, expensive oil paintings, and opulent decor and you'll have a pretty good idea of the feel of the 12th floor.

It was early morning and only two people were on the floor, Fred Stock, the Vice President of Marketing and Sales, and me. Fred told me how much he enjoyed his job and, in particular, how he relished tackling tough problems. He felt with appropriate justification that he was one of the few if not the only person on the floor who liked to come to work and who looked forward to making tough decisions.

To illustrate his point, Fred told me how he had talked the Squibb board into taking a chance on electric toothbrushes, in the face of significant opposition and derision. Why people would pay $20 for a toothbrush when they could get one for under $1, the board had asked. Fred had presented some very convincing arguments, and he closed the deal by offering up a challenge. He told the board that he was so sure he was right; he was willing to put his job on the line. If he turned out to be wrong, they should fire him. (The Broxident toothbrush was an unqualified success.)

On the surface, Fred seemed to be a supremely confident kind of guy. The truth was, he would not have had the courage to get the board to back down without his psychological crutch.

He confided to me that, what he called his "insurance policy" was hanging on the wall in the study at his home. This piece of paper gave him the courage to fight for what he thought was right, even when the stakes were high and the majority was against him. I remember how I couldn't wait to find out what this insurance policy was. Can you guess? I couldn't. It was a license to practice pharmacy in the state of Indiana.

To Fred, this license served as a psychological crutch an ego support system. He had never worked as a pharmacist nor had any intention of ever returning to Indiana to practice pharmacy. However, the fact was that under the worst of all circumstances, he could earn money and support his family. This fact gave him the confidence and the courage to do what he did.

Since that time I have come across dozens of similar types of psychological crutches (often impractical, illogical, or unrealistic) that many of us use from time to time to prop ourselves up and boost our self-confidence. In other words, one of the pillars of self-confidence is having a helpful illusion. What crutch do you use?

THEY LEARN HOW TO GET STROKES

The majority of us derive great intrinsic satisfaction from our accomplishments. You are certainly proud of what you've done. Furthermore, you want other people to appreciate and value your achievements. You want recognition, credit. You want strokes.

But, do you think you'll ever be fully appreciated? Will you always get the recognition you deserve? Will you get full credit for your contributions? I doubt it.

It's not easy to get the recognition and appreciation you deserve. You can whine about it, or you can do something about it. People with a higher level of self-esteem find ways to get credit (strokes) for what they've accomplished.

A survey conducted in one company found that most people felt they received less praise for their work than they deserved, and got more criticism. I've found this condition to be fairly universal. On a personal level, it dawned on me that if I wanted more strokes, I had to do something about it, I had to be proactive. Better to try to get more strokes than to complain about getting too much criticism and not enough praise. I decided the tennis court would be an ideal place to practice my skills in getting positive feedback.

If you had a video monitor of hundreds of social tennis games, you would frequently find an interesting sequence of events. Larry hits a great shot. Bob, his opponent, hits the return into the net. Bob then becomes highly self-critical, blaming himself for making a mistake. In this particular scenario the truth is that Bob did not lose the point Larry won the point with a great shot. Bob should not engage in self blame and Larry should get the credit for winning the point.

I'm sure you have already anticipated my new strategy for getting more strokes.

Whenever I made a great shot and my opponent got mad at himself, I'd stop the game. I'd go up to the net and say: "Hey! Instead of blaming yourself, why not give me credit for making a great shot?" The beauty of this technique was that it worked like a Pavlovian exercise. After I had stopped the game five or six times, my opponents became conditioned to a new set of responses.

Because this worked for tennis, I decided to try it in the business world. In a client meeting, I'd come up with an idea, and the client would say, "That's a good idea, Ed." And I'd lean over the desk and say "No, Jim, that's a great idea." Just as I learned how to get strokes, you can too. You have to figure out ways to get the credit you deserve, to give your ego the nourishment it needs.

In addition to learning better ways of getting strokes from others, you can boost your self-esteem by learning ways to give them to yourself.

For example, I often play tennis with a friend. He is far and away the better athlete: more competitive, in better shape, an all-around better player. When we play together, I normally lose, often badly. One time, though, I was just having a great day, while he was having a lousy one. It seemed that every shot I made was charmed, and every shot he made was cursed. I won our match, 61, 60, 61, and was so excited by this unheard of event that I did something you might find silly: I bought myself a trophy. It's a beauty: 12-inches-high, gold plated, with a figure of a person serving. On the base, I had a plate engraved with the date, my name, my opponent's name, and the score. It sits on one corner of my desk, where I can look at it and feel the boost that comes with remembering this rare accomplishment.

If no one will give me a trophy, I'll get my own.

How do you go about giving yourself a trophy? I know people who treat themselves to a night on the town, a nice dinner, or buy something that is outlandishly expensive. Just as you can be your own harshest critic, it's healthy to be your own biggest fan.

GAINING AND MAINTAINING SELF-CONFIDENCE IS A LIFETIME PROCESS

When I began working as a consultant for Merck & Company in 1963, the firm had 18,000 employees and posted $750 million in sales. At the time, Merck had products in its pipeline with the potential of fueling an enormous rate of growth. One of the first things I did for Merck was to perform an in-depth analysis of its pool of managerial talent. As a result, the top 600 managers went through two training programs.

In addition to these two basic programs, we also wanted to send selected leaders to appropriate courses offered by universities for upper level management executives.

I embarked on a fairly ambitious program to identify the best of these programs or the best professors we might invite to give seminars at the company's headquarters. I immediately began interviewing a large number of managers from other companies who had enrolled in courses sponsored by such schools as Harvard, MIT, Stanford and Carnegie Mellon. I asked them what they liked and what they didn't, which professors stood out in their minds, and whether or not they would recommend the course to others. And finally, the big question: what did they learn from the experience?

The results were surprising. Although I was looking for the best courses and instructors, what I found out was even more valuable. The main value of the courses, according to the trainees, was that they gained more confidence in themselves. The subject matter might have been marketing, acquisitions, long range planning or general management. Regardless of the content, the main benefit was an increase in the participant's self-esteem!

What actually happened? The individuals who went to a three week or six week training program at one of these topflight schools found themselves in a group of pretty impressive executives with big titles, big salaries and the responsibility for thousands of employees and millions of dollars. Each looked around the room the first day and had doubts that they would be able to keep up. But they kept up—to their surprise and relief—and their self-doubt diminished.

POINTS TO REMEMBER

When I conducted an in-depth analysis of individuals who had a great batting average in making choices, I found they had high ego-strength. What are some of the main points about them to remember?

- They Are Not Stampeded by the Herd.

- They Are Not Intimidated by Authority Figures.

- They Accept Their Genetically Fixed Advantages and Disadvantages.

- They Avoid Shooting Themselves in the Foot.

- They Learn to Trust Their Intuition.

- They Learn How to Get Strokes.

Core Attitudes of People with Common Sense

In many books on management, the prime emphasis is placed on competencies, i.e., to be successful you have to be decisive, or be good at setting priorities or be skilled as a communicator. These books minimize or neglect the importance of attitudes. In my studies, I found that the attitudes of a person have an enormous impact on their ability to achieve results, to earn a favorable reputation and to develop the best kind of working relationships. Individuals with common sense believe the following:

1. I will come out ahead by doing the right thing.

2. Anything worth doing is worth doing well.

3. I need all the brains I have and all I can borrow.

4. There is a sucker born every minute and I'm not going to be one.

5. Maintaining a positive attitude is essential.

6. There is more than one way to skin a cat.

(#3 was discussed in detail in Chapter 2. The importance of #5 is well understood and, I believe, requires no further elaboration.)

In addition to recognizing the incredible impact of attitudes, it is also important to keep in mind that they can be changed. One of the most preeminent American philosophers, William James (1842—1910) observed the following:

> *"The greatest discovery of my generation is that human beings can alter their lives by altering their attitudes."*

THEY WILL COME OUT AHEAD BY DOING THE RIGHT THINGS

Organizations are filled with people who different attitudes and these attitudes determine how they respond to different situations.

1. *Traditional* managers will favor the status quo or the way things have been done in the past. They always tell the younger people: "This company is very successful. Who are you to question the way we do things around here".

2. *Politicians* will look for the politically acceptable solution.

3. *The "Looking out for #1"* guys will favor the option which is in their best interests.

4. The *"I want to be liked"* type will work diligently to find a solution that irritates the fewest employees.

5. *Bureaucrats* are people whose sole purpose in life is to adhere to the rules and this attitude determines how they will deal with various situations.

People with common sense stand apart from the crowd because they consistently search for the right or best answer.

The precise definition of the "right" thing can vary depending on the situation. Sometimes, if you do the "right" thing by asking yourself what would be best if you owned the company. The "right" thing might be to do what is best over the long haul, even though problems will be created in the near term.. In some situations, involving personnel decisions, you need to ask yourself how you would wish to be treated if the roles were reversed. The "right" thing to do is often based on ethical considerations.

Strange as it may seem, when you are trying to do what is right, you will be right more often; you will respond to situations in an appropriate way.

ANYTHING WORTH DOING IS WORTH DOING WELL

If find the "right" answer to a problem is the first order of business, the second priority is to do the job right, to do it well, to do it in a professional manner. Doing things right is a matter of setting high standards. Individuals who achieve superior results, earn a superior reputation and establish a broad network of relationships hold themselves to a high standard. If they are building a building, they want it to be first-class. If they are putting together an advertising campaign, they want to do it in a highly professional way. If they are designing a product, they want to be proud of their work.

(It is unfortunate, in my opinion, that the basic idea of striving for excellence has, in recent times, become trivialized. Excellence is a word which is often found in corporate slogans and programs. There is quite a difference between those who give excellence lip service and those who instinctively set high standards for themselves.)

Vince Lombardi was one of the most famous of all professional football coaches. He became a role model for many successful business men, and was greatly admired for his competitive spirit. "Winning isn't everything, it's the only thing." was one of his most frequently quoted remarks.

Every Monday morning, Lombardi assembled the team to review a movie of the game played on Sunday. (This was before the era of TV.) Every time a mistake was made...the ball was fumbled, a tackle was missed, a block was done improperly...the film was stopped. Coach Lombardi then proceeded in no uncertain terms to explain to the wayward sinner the colossal nature of making such a stupid, idiotic, unforgivable error. In reporting on these postmortems, one of the players commented that, no mater whether you won or lost, there was no excuse for a below standard performance.

I think this is a great example of how individuals with high standards *have high expectations of themselves which goes hand in hand with having high expectations of others.*

The best managers make a special effort to maintain high standards when they are hiring or promoting people. Experience tells them that, when they lower their standards, they will always regret it. When you review the lives of successful people, it becomes very apparent that success was dependent on getting the right people in the right jobs. Gerstner summed it up very nicely when he said:

> "I try to set tough standards, hire the best people, and provide the incentive for them to do their best work." Lou Gerstner, former CEO of IBM

There Is a Sucker Born Every Minute and I'm Not Going to Be One

One attitude which clearly helps people make better choices is captured in the above quote of P.T. Barnum's. This attitude is vital if you are going to develop the ability to figure out whom to trust and the ability to be an effective risk taker.

When you are skeptical, you make better choices which results in improvements in your relationships, reputation and results.

A Core Attitude—Skepticism

**You Make
Better Choices**

**You Check and Cross Check
Your Information to be Sure
It is Both Valid and Complete**

**Your Relationships
Reputation and
Results Improve**

> THERE IS A SUCKER BORN
> EVERY MINUTE AND I AM
> NOT
> GOING TO BE ONE OF THEM

There Is More Than One Way to Skin a Cat

Finally, the best people are resourceful. Resourcefulness is based on an attitude, captured by the axiom: "*There is more than one way to skin a cat.*" If they encounter a wall, they try to dig under it. If that doesn't work, they try to go around it or get a ladder and go over it. If all else fails, they might resort to dynamite. Meanwhile, the more rigid people keep batting their heads against the wall.

Jack Miller was the plant manager of an alumina plant in Baton Rouge. When he took over, the plant had one of the worst safety records of any plant in the corporation. He tried all the conventional, logical approaches to improving safety—intensive communications with employees about the importance of safety, setting goals for decreased lost time due to accidents, conducting training programs, following safety engineers' recommendations, rewarding people for good safety records. Nothing had really helped. Jack persisted.

In this plant, one of the rules was that everyone had to wear a hard hat. People in different departments wore different colored hats: engineers had blue hats, operations people had white hats, etc. Jack had them make one black hat. In the center of the hat there was a black billiard ball with the number eight printed in white. At a certain point in a game of billiards, making a short when the cue ball is behind the eight ball is extremely difficult. "Behind the eight ball" is a slang expression, meaning a place where you don't want to be.

The next time there was an accident, the foreman of that group had to wear the black hat until another accident occurred. *No one wanted to be stuck wearing the black ha*t, so all the foremen redoubled their efforts to be sure no one in their group had an accident. The plant, in a very short period of time, surpassed all its safety goals.

POINTS TO REMEMBER

Attitudes can be changed and they determine outcomes. Individuals who have good judgment believe the following:

1. **I will come out ahead by doing the right thing.**

2. **Anything worth doing is worth doing well.**

3. **I need all the brains I have and all I can borrow.**

4. **There is a sucker born every minute and I'm not going to be one.**

5. **Maintaining a positive attitude is essential.**

6. **There is more than one way to skin a cat.**

Section 4

Humor

o o o o o o o o o o o o o o o o o o o o o o o o o o o o o o o o o

"Do not take life too seriously.
You will never get out of it alive!"

—*Hubbard*

A Tour Guide of the Industrial Zoo

Some of the individuals in your organization have an innate ability to frustrate, annoy, and perplex you. They don't always act in a rational way. They do not handle situations the right way (i.e., the way *you* handle them). This state of affairs isn't good for your mental health. Their actions tend to upset your psychological equilibrium...your internal harmony. When this happens, you are not at your best. Your blood pressure increases, you take out your frustration on your family or friends, and it is generally a downhill trip.

When people don't act in a rational way, don't handle things the right way, and are not as consistent and predictable as they should be, you ask yourself: "Why is this person doing such and such?" This question leads you to a dead end. You begin to speculate about people's motives. You wonder about the cause of their behavior. Do they have an excessive need for control, are they are overcompensating, or do they feel threatened?

Does this line of questioning help you significantly? Absolutely not, because "Why?" is an enormously helpful question in many situations, such as, "Why won't my car start?" But most of the time "Why?" is the worst question to ask when you are trying to understand someone's behavior. When you speculate about the origins of a person's behavior, there is no way to prove your analysis is correct. You are guessing. You can never be 100 percent sure that you have found the right explanation, so you end up back where you started, annoyed, irritated, and so forth.

You must make a paradigm shift. To protect your inner harmony and achieve a better understanding of people, you must adopt a different frame of reference. Fortunately, there is a readymade answer to your dilemma. You have to use your imagination and think of people around you as various kinds of other animals. When you do that, you should dramatically improve your ability to predict behavior—one of the key talents of people with common sense.

We never try to figure out why an eagle flies or why a fish swims. The eagle flies and the fish swim because of natural selection and random mutations. Humans are one species of the animal world. They also have genetic programs. They do what comes naturally. They are guided by their instincts. If we understand the different kinds of instincts, we may end up being less confused or puzzled, therefore, spending less energy searching for answers that lie right in front of us.

You be the judge. As you read these pages, I think you will come away with an entirely different point of view about people. When you think of people as other kinds of animals, it is simple. If an animal walks like a duck, quacks like a duck, and looks like a duck, the chances are very good that he, she, or it is a duck.

We often compare people's actions with the behavior of other animals. We talk about people who are "strong as an ox," "quiet as a mouse," or "stubborn as a mule." Some people charge ahead oblivious to the damage they cause. We say they are like a "bull in a china shop." When you have a hard, driving, ambitious person working for you, you tell your friends you have a "tiger by the tail."

THE PORCUPINE

The Porcupine is the only one who ever flunked the Dale Carnegie Course. When you meet someone who automatically offends, irritates, and antagonizes you, you have met a Porcupine. Porcupines rub people the wrong way. It would be more accurate to say they prick you with barbed comments. They literally "get under your skin." They have a special, well-honed talent for alienating people.

I once met a high-level executive who made more disparaging, insulting, contemptuous, and abrasive comments in one hour than most people make in a whole year while he was trying to be polite.

One of the fascinating attributes of Porcupines is their total lack of awareness of the impact of their behavior. When they are confronted with the fact that they have irritated people, they are completely unable to fathom what they could have said that was offensive.

Porcupines don't offend simply by jabbing people with quills. They are more versatile than that. For example, in a meeting, they can make you feel inadequate by completely ignoring your comments. This is the "I'll-make-you-feel-bad-because-you-aren't-important" gambit. They use the same approach when they don't even say hello to people they pass in the hall. Porcupines are just doing what comes naturally. You should not take their insults personally because nothing personal is intended. They are equal opportunity offenders.

THE PEACOCK

In every company and every social gathering, there are one or more Peacocks strutting their stuff. They are exhibitionists. They're completely self-centered and self-absorbed. When a sense of humility was being issued in the supply room in the sky, the Peacock was playing hooky. As listeners, on a scale from one to ten, they get a minus five, except when nice things are being said about them. The word they use most frequently is not surprisingly "I."

When they wake up every morning, they look at themselves in a full length mirror and do their recitation of the refrain from a book for children: "Mirror, Mirror, on the wall, who is the fairest one of all?" It is most entertaining to watch them play tennis. They stand perfectly still, waiting for the ball to come to them. And they feel insulted if it doesn't. After all, they are the center of everything, and therefore they expect the ball to be pulled to them by some kind of centrifugal force. Their parents must have convinced them that they were the center of the universe.

THE FAST-THINKING ELEPHANT

There is a rare breed of elephant found in the distant regions of the Himalayas whose excellent memory is matched by the speed with which they can do mathematical calculations. This is indeed a formidable combination.

Elephants don't forget anything. They remember the memorandum you wrote four years ago on April the 2nd. They remember the offhand comment you made at a cocktail party. If you have been too optimistic, they don't forget it, nor do they forget when you've been too pessimistic. Every promise you ever made is stored in their mental data bank. Their memory is admirable, astonishing, and amazing! On the other hand, it is also annoying, alienating, and aggravating. They aggravate you because you lose debates when they recall an overwhelming number of facts to support their arguments, even when they are wrong. Arguing with an Elephant is like playing double solitaire against an opponent with a full deck when you have half a deck.

They also aggravate you because you can never supply enough details to satisfy them. Details, whether relevant or not, are like peanuts they love to devour. When you write a report for an Elephant, it is standard procedure to include a hefty appendix filled with facts, figures, and footnotes.

Not only do these special elephants have tremendous recall, they are also able to make calculations with amazing rapidity. They can quickly scan pages of numbers and spot any inconsistencies, errors, or underlying trends. Their mental machinery automatically converts raw numbers into ratios and percentages.

Any contest between an Elephant and a normal person is lopsided, unfair, and therefore "un-American." Fair-minded Elephants should adopt a strategy designed to put other people on equal footing, instead of sandbagging them, Elephants should begin a meeting by saying something like: "I have had a chance to review the report. I'm sure that all of you are aware that sales and constant dollars have decreased only 10% each year compounded annually over the last five years. Promotional spending, when allowances have been made for the increase in media rates, and the rise of the cost of printing has increased 15.4%. Let's start the discussion based on these facts." In this way they can bring everybody in the room to the same starting point.

THE PONDEROUS ELEPHANT

The second kind of elephant is the ponderous Elephant. These are people who are locked into one speed: slow. Your impatience or sense of urgency about the matter does not move them. They are cautious, prudent and careful, but they have the advantage of being highly predictable. Predictability has its virtues when you are coping with a world of uncertainty.

THE GULL

Gulls are interesting birds. When you watch them fly they seem to defy the laws of gravity. Regardless of the wind direction or intensity, they always are able to maintain their balance and poise. They float and glide their way from one problem to another as if the problems were telephone poles. For them a problem is not something they want to solve, it's just a temporary resting place. Since they do not solve problems, they do not make any mark on the organization. They aren't trying to make a mark: they are just trying to stay up in the air.

THE METAMORPHOSIS OF LIONS

I am sure you are familiar with Eager Beavers, Tigers, and Lions. They must be viewed as steps in a progression. When we took biology in high school, we learned about many things we could not apply and have since forgotten. Most of us however, remember about the metamorphosis of the butterfly. The caterpillar emerges from the butterfly egg. When the caterpillar reaches its full growth, it turns into a pupa. Finally, the adult butterfly emerges.

Some people pass through a similar kind of metamorphosis. Eager Beavers become Tigers before being transformed into Lions. Eager Beavers are anxious to prove themselves and please their superiors. They are enthusiastic, optimistic, and impatient to make their mark on the world. They are highly industrious and take on more work than they can reasonably accomplish. They have made up their minds that they will "pay the price," whatever it is, to get ahead. Like their counterpart who builds dams in the wilderness, Eager Beavers are bright-eyed and bushy tailed.

Some people have suggested that workaholics are brain-damaged Eager Beavers. As Eager Beavers are encouraged, promoted, and given more responsibility they become Tigers who lash their tails, snarl, and stalk the object of their desire. They become ferocious when opposed. In manufacturing they prowl the factory floor on a constant vigil for ways to cut costs. In sales, they growl at their people about quotas.

When Tigers develop a middle-aged paunch, and progress into top management, they make their entrance into the ranks of Lions. Lions are tired Tigers. When they were younger they were ferocious and roared when they meant business. Lions roar not because they really mean it but because they just enjoy roaring. It is a happy habit. Also, they don't want to forget that they were once Tigers.

Lions are mellowed by modern day comforts, such as the company airplane and elegant hotel suites. They are treated with the kind of deference they have always wanted but did not possess as Tigers. Their dens have thick carpets and wood-paneled walls. Lions are not as combative as they were when they were younger. Because they are fiercely loyal, they will fight when they need to protect their subordinates.

THE FOX

Contrary to popular belief, foxes are not necessarily bad guys. Immortalized by Walt Disney cartoon characters, they are depicted to be devious, cunning, and tricky characters that we hope will "outfox" themselves. Foxes have not been treated very kindly in literature or in cartoons. To understand foxes, we must view some of their attributes, which are frequently cast in a negative light, and see them as redeeming, if not admirable, characteristics.

Instead of looking at them as devious, their actions can be viewed as clever and strategically appropriate. Cunning acts also can be sensibly shrewd. The person who is tricky in one light is often considered ingenious and resourceful in another.

Foxes can be bold, adventurous risk takers. They can extricate themselves from a seemingly impossible predicament by outsmarting the opposition. They can compensate for a lack of strength by intellectual brilliance. In many situations, Foxes will succeed where others have failed. "The Prince," wrote Niccolo Machiavelli, "must imitate the Fox and the Lion for the Lion cannot protect himself from traps and the Fox cannot defend himself from the wolves. One must therefore be a Fox to recognize traps and a Lion to frighten wolves."

THE GIRAFFE

Giraffes are one of the most frustrated of all animals. Standing high above the crowd, they have a different point of view. They cannot see what is going on close at hand, so they don't get enmeshed in the crisis du jour. Instead they have a glimpse of what lies ahead. They are visionaries. Since almost everyone possesses hindsight, it should be noted that the gift of foresight is possessed only by a handful of people. Giraffes are majestically lonely figures. Since they see what other people cannot see, they are always ahead of their time. And, like a sighted person trying to describe something to a blind man, Giraffes have real communication problems. The most rewarding experience the Giraffe can have is to find a non-giraffe who is willing to listen and who wants to learn what the Giraffe is able to see.

THE BULLDOGS

The one and only distinguishing characteristic of some people is their unwillingness to give up. They carry tenacity and persistence to the outer limits. When a sale is made, instead of writing up the order, they continue to sell and manage to convince the customer not to buy. When a decision has been made that goes contrary to their wishes, they infuriate everyone because they continue to argue. Even when commanded to cease and desist they will not stop. They are Bulldogs.

If a Bulldog were in command of a submarine that had been fatally damaged in battle and was sinking rapidly to the bottom of the ocean, he would continue to fire torpedoes. Religious Bulldogs are the most difficult breed to handle. When you suggest a compromise, they think you are asking them to violate their moral principles. They cause special problems when they have Quality Control responsibilities.

There are two other types of dogs worth mentioning. The Show Dog makes superb presentations, giving brilliant, sometimes dazzling presentations to upper management. However, all they are good for is the show: they are inept when it comes to execution. The Work Dog gets things done, but often don't show well.

THE OWL

Every organization has one or two Owls. Owls never move to great heights in organizations because they prefer contemplation to action. You never meet young owls. It requires years of experience and seasoning to acquire wisdom, which is the hallmark of the Owl. Owls are tolerant, understanding and able to put things in perspective. Their counsel is sound and never self-serving. They like to teach and share their knowledge with young people. They have the kind of detachment that is characteristic of good advisors and mentors.

THE TURTLE

The Turtle never inspired anybody to write a book and call it *Jonathan Livingston Turtle*. Instead of having strong and maneuverable wings, the turtle has its shell. The shell is colored so it blends unobtrusively into the surroundings. Faced with conflict and frightened by new ideas or confronted by a tough decision, Turtles retreat into their shells. When the coast is clear, they stick their head out again, but not very far. Turtles never make mistakes because they don't take risks. It is always comforting to have people around who don't make errors, as long as they're not expected to take chances.

THE WORKHORSE

Some people in organizations produce a tremendous amount of work with little fanfare. They stick to the job at hand. They wear blinders so they can concentrate totally on the task before them without being distracted by gossip, rumors, and petty office politics. They have no illusions of grandeur or unrealistic ambitions. They only expect a fair day's pay for doing a good job. They rarely antagonize other people and command considerable respect. They avoid the limelight. They are Workhorses.

THE WATER BUFFALO

In business, I respect the old Water Buffaloes. They have a "survival of the fittest ability" that only comes from a history of combat experience with different adversaries and on different battlegrounds. They've won some battles and lost others. They wear their share of battle scars so they don't look very glamorous and often do not make very good first impressions.

THE TURKEY

It has been said that there are four kinds of people in companies: (1) those that make things happen; (2) the people who have things happen to them; (3) those who watch while things are happening; and (4) those who don't even know that something is happening. The last group are the Turkeys. The Turkeys were bypassed when smarts were being handed out. So, unfortunately, they generally do not understand what is happening, and if they finally catch on it's too late. Wild Turkeys cause a commotion when they are alarmed because they scurry around, flapping their wings and making peculiar noises. The conventional wisdom is you can't fly like an Eagle if you're surrounded by Turkeys.

THE DONKEY

Some people are so stubborn and inflexible it becomes a chore to work with them. They severely test your patience. If you threaten them they ignore you. The kind and understanding approach also fails. All the best reasons will not get them to shift their position. You will have to hit them over the head with a two by four to get their attention, but you only get their attention momentarily. They will then resume their previous direction. Every manager has subordinates and insubordinates: the latter are the Donkeys.

THE SHEEP

The Sheep, as a subordinate, is a complete opposite of the Donkey. Sheep are pliable and suggestible. They were born to be followers and not leaders. They will follow anyone. They rarely complain or make a fuss and consistently do what they are told. If you have been around Donkeys, Sheep must have a certain appeal for you. However, Sheep won't stand up to you when you are wrong and you need someone who can point out your error. A Sheep is a "yes man" in a wool coat.

THE POMPOUS PENGUIN

You certainly know people who are stuffed shirts. They are the ones who are always formal and proper. They cannot bend or relax. They treat you in a condescending manner, as if they are in fact superior to you. They do not become angry or emotional because they are somehow detached and above it all. While they know all the correct rules of etiquette, they lack the ability to be flexible and lighthearted. Pompous Penguins are aloof, distant and cool.

◆   ◆   ◆

It is impossible to review the entire animal kingdom. You probably are familiar with some breeds that I have not encountered or mentioned. I should, however, just mention some of the relatively rare, but noteworthy, species.

- Kangaroos jump so frequently that their administrative assistants never know where to locate them.

- Hornets always seem to be mad at someone.

- Ostriches stay calm by sticking their heads in the sand.

- Parrots repeat what other people say without adding any value.

- Squids constantly muddy the water.

- Bluebirds of Happiness are sure everything is going to turn out for the best.

- Crabs are constantly complaining.

- Thoroughbred Horses often kick the slats of their stalls upsetting people.

- Mountain goats leap from one crisis to another.

Too many managers make the mistake of trying to get a person to perform some kind of task which not a part of their talent repertoire. Keep in mind the saying:

Meetings Can Be the High Point of Your Day

Most business executives are frustrated by both the quality and quantity of the meetings that they attend each week. This universal sense of frustration is in itself significant. However, it is even more significant that managers must spend more and more time in meetings and, consequently, have less and less time for productive work. You may have felt that you go to so many that you don't have enough time left to get your work done.

The ultimate authority on management, Peter Drucker, says, "Meetings by definition are a concession to deficient organization. For one either meets or works. One cannot do both at the same time."

I am going to present a compelling argument that all companies should totally change the approach to meetings. Meetings should never be held to achieve some business objective. Instead, they should be thought of as a way to reduce employee stress. If this can be achieved meetings will be exciting rather than dull, challenging rather than boring, invigorating rather than lifeless. Everyone will look forward to attending.

AGGRAVATIONS AND IRRITATIONS

Complaints about meetings are too varied and numerous to enable me to set forth a complete list of them. Here is a short list:

- Attended by the wrong people.

- Attended by too many people.

- Attended by people who are not prepared.

- Purpose is poorly defined.

- Leader or chairperson is inept.

- Take too long.

- Innumerable digressions impede progress.

- The people who have the least to contribute usually monopolize most of the time.

To the mentally alert, the signals are clear that there is room for improvement.

I am quite sure that you would not take exception to the above statements. You have direct experience that is consistent with what I have said. Apart from your experience, it might interest you to know what various authors have said about committees.

- A committee is a group of the unprepared appointed by the unwilling to do the unnecessary.

- Nothing is ever accomplished by committee unless it consists of three members, one of whom happens to be sick and the other absent.

- A committee is a group that keeps the minutes and loses hours.

- In the history of mankind, there has never been a statue erected to commemorate a committee.

(The authors are either unknown or it has been difficult to determine the originator.)

All these quotations preceded Power Point, which has elevated the absurdity of meetings to a much higher level. The presenter comes in, not with an executive summary, but an encyclopedia of all the information you don't need to know. Then, they spend ten minutes reading the material displayed on a slide which members of the audience can read in five seconds. Doesn't it insult your intelligence when someone reads to you as if you were in the first grade and is thereby wasting an enormous amount of your time?

THE SHOCKING UNINTENDED CONSEQUENCES

So what? It is clear to all of us that there are too many meetings, but what are the consequences? Do companies suffer from having so many meetings? Is there a negative impact on profits? The negative organizational consequences are minimal. Does that surprise you?

The mission of any corporation is to compete successfully. Since your competitors hold as many foolish meetings as you do, no firm is disadvantaged. It is a level playing field.

What are the never before disclosed and frightfully negative consequences? Read on!

Since people attend so many meetings they cannot get their work done, what do they do? They take work home with them all the time. In my opinion, this is the real reason for the decay in family values in the U.S.! Seems the rule, rather than the exception, is for both the mother and father to work. When they have to bring work home with them, there is no time to give children the proper guidance or to instill the right values.

Consequently, the kids take drugs; they drop out of school, and go on welfare. The results is that the national debt balloons, Congress cannot balance the budget, central banks could lose confidence in the value of the dollar, worldwide currencies might plummet, and the result could be a global depression.

All because there are too darn many meetings.

There you have it! Excess meetings are not simply a waste of time and the cause of enormous irritation and aggravation, they also can create an international crisis!

MEETINGS ARE HELD FOR THE WRONG REASONS

Clearly, this problem is well worth a national crusade to help us prevent having a global depression. To solve the problem, we must delve into its basic causes. Why do meetings cause so much trouble? The basic cause is quite simple...groups meet for the wrong reasons. By closely examining the reasons for meetings, we can gain insight into why corrective action is needed.

The justification of any meeting is that it is designed to achieve some purpose that will benefit the company or organization.

The three purported purposes are:

1. To exchange information.

2. To arrive at a decision.

3. To improve cooperation between groups or individuals.

Superficially, these seem to be solid, legitimate reasons for people to get together. Managers do need to exchange information; decisions must be made; and, of course, cooperation is necessary for success. On the surface, the orthodox reasons for people to meet appear to be sensible but, as we shall see, there is a gigantic difference between the theory and the facts.

THE FALLACY OF INFORMATION EXCHANGE

The intent of a meeting at which information is exchanged is not difficult to comprehend. Different people have different pieces of information about any given problem. John's data adds to Jane's knowledge and she, in turn, reveals some marvelously significant fact unknown to Pat. Through such a chain reaction, it should be possible to create a group synergism that elicits a total exchange of information. One would think this would be spectacularly superior to the pool of information available to any single person who is limited by such normal handicaps as a limited point of view, a partly defective memory, or a tendency to believe what one wants to believe.

Does the information exchange session fulfill these expectations?

One company held 100 sessions whose stated purpose was the exchange of information; these meetings were tape-recorded. The tapes were transcribed, and the contents of each discussion were analyzed. It was possible to identify six types of activities that occurred during these sessions.

PERCENTAGE OF TIME SPENT BY TYPE OF ACTIVITY

20% Recyclying of known information	Discussions about items that were known to the participants prior to the session. This is usually known as belavoring the obvious.
19% Reiteration of personal prejudice	Individuals restated biases and prejudices that, on number occasions, had been expressed previously. Naturally, nobody listened.
18% Criticisms of those not present	Individuals from other departments, or those higher or lower in the hierarchy than the group members, were publicly castigated for poor leadership, incompetence, stupidity, dishonesty, and other minor failures or flaws.
17% Gossip	Implications of rumored or recent organization changes, items of interest from the world of sports, and views on sex, the generation gap, and politics, were discussed.
16% In-depth analysis of the irrelevant	Time was spent in extended conversation covering small details about minor matters of little consequence.

As we can see from the results of this study, the noble and lofty aspirations of this type of session are not potent enough to prevent people from doing what comes naturally and easily (i.e., criticizing other people, gossiping, fleeing from the core of a problem to its periphery, digressing, etc.).

WHAT IS THE ROLE OF A MEETING IN THE DECISION-MAKING PROCESS?

According to conventional wisdom, you get people together to make decisions. As is usually the case, we cannot take the conventional wisdom as gospel.

Although a meeting can be held to create the illusion of participation in a decision, decisions are not made by groups. Groups don't have authority. Individuals have authority. If the executive who has the authority needs some input, he or she can pick up the phone and get the information rather than hold a meeting.

(The exception is the U.S. Congress, which has the authority to make a decision by taking a vote. However, no self-respecting company wants to use the Congress of the United States as a role model.)

DO MEETINGS ENHANCE COLLABORATION, COOPERATION, AND TEAMWORK?

The third kind of meeting—the one designed to achieve cooperation and collaboration between individuals and groups—is the phoniest of the lot, and we shall waste little time exposing it.

Common sense tells us that uncooperative, stubborn, and argumentative people were born that way, and getting them together with the idea that the level of cooperation will be improved is like expecting water to run uphill.

Similarly, in the DNA of organizations, we all know that functional groups are natural enemies. For example, it is often the case that the people in Sales make foolish concessions to customers that drive the Manufacturing costs completely out of line. If the Salespeople were allowed to have their way, the company would be bankrupt in no time. It is the solemn and duty-bound function of Manufacturing to prevent that from happening. How can anyone expect a meeting to change this state of affairs?

Human Resources, Finance, Operations, Sales, Marketing, Engineering, Information Services, and R&D are all inevitable antagonists. Therefore, meetings whose purported purpose is to get people to act like they are working for the same company are doomed to fail.

In summary, all the evidence conclusively shows that meetings do not achieve their intended purpose whatever the purpose happens to be.

THE BASIC ERROR

Based on the foregoing analysis, it should be perfectly clear that there is something fundamentally wrong with most meetings. The error involved is so basic and simple that, up to now, it has been completely overlooked.

The mechanism of choice for resolving key organization issues is usually not a meeting.

USING THE INFORMAL NETWORK TO GET INFORMATION

We have already seen the results of the research study showing that in a typical meeting only ten percent of the time was spent on a discussion of new and useful information. This is clearly inefficient. The solution is simple.

We all know that the best sources of information come from informal networks.

All we have to do is encourage employees to redouble their efforts in doing what they already do. They must seek out the most reliable sources of information that can help them do their job better. This list would include limo drivers, some very low level (but very well informed) employees in Human Resources, the boss's secretary, and others who are really "in the know."

If you are well wired, there is very little need to hold a meeting or attend one. But, when your sources fail you, then and only then, should you call a meeting. I believe that a meeting should be the mechanism of last resort.

IMPROVING DECISION-MAKING

Meetings often happen because authority is not being properly delegated. The way to improve decision-making is to delegate both authority and responsibility—a novel concept in most organizations. No mater how difficult, it must be done. The principles regulating the delegation of authority are simple, and are discussed extensively in the literature on management. They should not need to be restated here.

IMPROVING COLLABORATION

Improving collaboration requires a two-prong strategy.

Short term, we have to focus on current employees. Long term, we have to modify the hiring practices to be sure we hire cooperative people.

To address the first issue, we need to get a list of uncooperative people. This is easy to do. Select 25 people at random. Send them a questionnaire to be returned unsigned. Ask them to list five people who are primary obstructionists (i.e., those individuals who throw sand in the machinery of progress). From this sample, select the top twelve.

We will call this list The Dirty Dozen, a group of people who are determined to protect their own empires, oppose progress, and resist any change. These people should be assigned to a colony of misfits, and should be left in this group until they prove capable of normal cooperation.

All members of the misfit colony of Dirty Dozen should be required to wear purple armbands. Their parking spaces should be the ones most distant from the office. Most importantly, they should be required to eat at one special table in the lunchroom. (It is indeed amazing how cooperative people can become after extended exposure to others who mirror their own undesirable attributes). Periodically, a survey should be taken and the group reconstituted.

The next step is to change the hiring practices. As a prime requisite for employment, you want team players.

All applicants should be carefully screened. Potential obstructionists should be immediately eliminated. An effective and simple approach, which is used rarely, is to have a hypnotist perform the screening. Job applicants who are difficult to hypnotize are excessively rigid and uncommonly stubborn—not the right profile of a team player.

MEETINGS DESIGNED TO IMPROVE MENTAL HEALTH

Because we now have a way to eliminate nonproductive meetings and replace them with effective strategies for achieving corporate objectives, the natural question is whether all meetings should be abolished? Absolutely not!

Although they fail to achieve the three organizational goals, meetings satisfy many psychological needs. This is why the number of meetings continues to proliferate even though everyone recognizes that they are a big waste of time, and that efforts to reduce the number of meetings are doomed to failure.

As companies have built gyms and spent considerable time and money in efforts to create a more physically healthy workforce, they also need to spend equal effort in developing an emotionally healthy work force. Meetings are a splendid way to accomplish such an objective. All organizations should have meetings designed to have some psychotherapeutic advantage—to give employees the opportunity to gratify various psychic needs.

What are some of these needs?

1. The Need to Belong

Those individuals who join a large company want to belong. If they didn't, they would have opened a newspaper stand, or a shoe shop, and earned a living in a respectable fashion. It is the nature of people to be gregarious. They want companionship. Part of the value of their job is that it puts them into contact with others.

This herd instinct is strong and cannot be denied. It explains why solitary confinement is such a dreaded and drastic punishment. It also explains why meetings are so necessary to maintain appropriate mental health in an organization.

2. The Need to Escape

The need to escape from the drudgery of work is a very basic and compelling human instinct (note the increase of television viewing). People don't naturally and spontaneously like to create budgets or year plans or monthly reports. They don't like to write long reports that are inevitably ignored.

The need to have an escape hatch, to break the routine, and to remove oneself from the tedious detail of work, that pervades all companies. A meeting can be like a Coca Cola—it is the pause that refreshes.

3. The Need to Complain, Blame, Feel Sorry for Oneself

We all know that when we are able to have some kind of catharsis, we not only feel better but also can attack our work with renewed vigor.

4. The Exhibitionist Urge

The gratification that comes from having an audience started when our parents applauded us for learning to talk and walk. Although we constantly search for and never find an audience as good as our parents, a group meeting provides us with a stage for our act. (As a side observation, it is interesting to note that good listeners are in short supply and the reason might be that parents continually praise and reward children for learning how to talk, but no child gets a lollipop for being a good listener.)

CONCLUSIONS

At the beginning of this chapter, there is a very long list of the problems excessive meetings create for managers. Now, we are in the happy position of making a long list of the advantages that will flow from holding meetings not for organizational reasons, but to provide employees a better way to gratify some basic psychological needs.

- Employees will not have to take work home.

- Children will be taught sound values and they will become better students and grow up to get good jobs. Drug use will drop, welfare rolls will diminish, and payroll tax payments to the government will increase.

- The national debt will disappear. Bankers all over the world will have confidence in the dollar.

- We will avoid the horrible prospects of a worldwide depression.

The One-Trait One-Question
Interview Method

It is possible for you, by religiously following one simple rule, to consistently hire and promote outstanding people who will be a credit to you and your organization. You can hire people who are sure to succeed and, better yet, will succeed where others have failed. You will have more time to shop, play golf, bet on the ponies, collect art, or indulge in whatever turns you on.

In general terms, this rule requires you to eliminate all candidates who lack one specific trait and to hire only those who have it. It is a one-trait system. This means it is necessary to disregard all factors other than the one trait.

Needless to say, this is a revolutionary concept. The idea is to totally disregard the conventional wisdom that stresses finding people with the right work experience, with certain educational qualifications, and who fit your culture. In rare cases, your ideal candidate could turn out to have limited experience in your industry and, like many other successful people, only a high school education.

A revolutionary concept deserves to be matched by a revolutionary method of implementation. A simple method has been perfected. To discover this one trait, it is necessary to ask only one question. The prime objective, of course, is to hire people that will give you a competitive advantage. The one question method happens to have many other side benefits. Think of the time you will save. As you perfect this method, the entire interview should take approximately fifteen minutes.

Not only will you require less time but also you will dramatically increase the efficiency of the interviewing process. Both the interviewers and the interviewees tend to be busy people with heavy work and travel schedules. Arranging a mutually convenient time for meeting turns into a nightmare. Using the one question method, you can screen out a large number of applicants with telephone interviews.

Finally, the biggest advantage to this approach is that it takes the guess-work out of the interviewing process, a process best captured by the one-time chief of the U.S. Employment service, who said:

> The employment interview as it is usually conducted is a matter of making extensive inferences about complex variables based on inade-quate data obtained in artificial situations, by unqualified observers.

To convert to the one-trait one-question system you must be willing to forsake your present hiring strategy, which is probably some version of the three systems which are in vogue at the present time: the Superman-Won-der Woman strategy, the clone strategy, and the stress interview.

THE SUPERMAN—WONDER WOMAN STRATEGY

The Superman—Wonder Woman strategy starts with someone listing the qualities of the ideal candidate for some senior level position. As we will see, this approach initially appears to be logical and sensible, however, it inevitably leads to picking people on a random basis.

The ideal candidate should leap tall buildings in a single bound, be faster than a speeding bullet, walk on water, and talk to God. They need to be as good at global strategy as they are in execution. They must be charis-matic leaders. They should have advanced degrees in law, science, and finance and mastery of a few languages is desirable. The ideal candidate is perfect. Since everyone knows all the shortcomings of the top people in the company and there are no perfect people, all internal candidates are ruled out. Then, the company hires an executive recruiting firm to con-duct a search

In practice, when this method is utilized, what happens?

Some person who appears to be ideal is hired, but they don't last long because it turns out their shortcomings are more serious than those of the internal candidates. Or, the interviewers cannot find an applicant who measures up to the list of qualifications. As a result, their level of frustration intolerance increases to an unacceptable level. When that happens, they hire the next applicant. So, if the interviewer has a low level of tolerance, they will hire the fifth applicant. If they have a little higher level of tolerance, they hire the tenth applicant. If they are unusually persistent, they hire the fifteenth applicant. What has happened? The selection process has become employment by roulette.

THE CLONE STRATEGY

The cloning strategy is much easier to execute because there is very little frustration, and it is even enjoyable. There is a natural and normal tendency to hire in our own image. Everyone knows people who went to Yale hire Yale graduates and people with engineering backgrounds hire other engineers, and ex-military officers hire comrades-in-arms.

The point is that we should not hire people who are like us, but people who complement us. So, the Cloning Strategy is designed to produce a result just the opposite of what is most desirable.

THE STRESS INTERVIEW

Admiral Rickover, the father of the nuclear submarine, had the front two legs of a chair shortened. When an officer was being interviewed for a promotion, he was constantly in danger of sliding off the chair. Various techniques were derived from this approach, but they all failed. The tactics of the interviewer were so apparent that the best applicants were turned off and sought employment elsewhere.

None of these strategies work.

THE ULTIMATE ANSWER

There is only one thing to look for in a job applicant. There is one trait that alone can readily compensate for any and all of the person's deficiencies. All the experience and talent of an applicant may end up having not much value if this trait is lacking. It is a trait that is more genetic than developed. There is no way to tell from a resume whether a person has it or not. That trait is luck. Luck is like height; it is a matter of genetics. If we pick 10,000 people at random and plot the distribution of their heights, we will get a bell-shaped curve. A large number of people are average, some are below average, and some are above. The same is true with luck.

People from many different cultures throughout history have recognized the monumental importance of luck.

In the Old Testament, paraphrasing Ecclesiastes, "The race is not to the swift, nor the battle to the strong, but you can bet your bottom dollar that the luckiest person will be the victor every time."

A Russian proverb from the fifth century asserts, "If you were born lucky, even your rooster will lay eggs."

An Italian philosopher proclaimed that with luck on your side, you could do without brains.

An Arab piece of folklore contends that if you throw a lucky person into the Nile, they will come up with a fish in their mouth.

To determine whether a person is lucky or not we should follow the example of the president of a company who had three applicants for the top financial job. He asked each of them only one question. The question was, "How much is two and two?" Two of the applicants said the answer was four. The person who got the job said, "Did you have some number in mind?"

I think we can profitably piggyback on this experience and ask a prospective applicant only one question. "Do you consider yourself to be a lucky person?" With experience, you will find that people will respond to this question in one of several ways.

Some people will get a glazed look in their eyes. So you have their answer before they've even said a word, for their actions speak louder than any words. They get a glazed look because they have never even considered the role of luck in their lives. The lucky person...the person you are looking for...always recognizes and appreciates the fact that their success is due in part to their good luck.

In these cases, you want to terminate the interview as quickly and politely as possible. If the person doesn't appreciate something as basic and fundamental as the role of luck, it is difficult to imagine how many other basic things they do not understand.

There is another kind of person who, when asked about being lucky, immediately begins to tell you their sad tale of woe. Their life is a history of bad breaks. They got a good job, had to relocate, and shortly thereafter, the company went bankrupt. Or, they worked for one company for fifteen years, relocating five times and each time they lost a sizable amount of money because the real estate market moved in the wrong direction. They bought a new car and the next day parked it at the mall, only for someone to ram into it.

At the end of the interview, you advise the applicant that you would really like to hire them but you do not have a position that pays enough to attract them. You tell them you certainly don't want to offer them a job that would be an insult to their great talents. You go on to say that there are other companies that are hiring at the present time, and then give the applicant the name and phone number of the competitor who has been taking market share away from you. In some cases, where this approach is used to good advantage, the competitor might be hiring ten or twenty unlucky people while you are only hiring the luckiest people. That is what we call an honest-to-goodness competitive advantage.

Then there is the type who says: "I don't believe in luck." They proceed to lecture to you about their success being based on a dedication to work, excellent people skills, and their ability to make swift and sure decisions. In short, they suffer from the advanced stages of a crippling disease, megalomania. If you hire them and they get to know you, they might end up thinking they are better than you are!

Another kind of person says, "Would you define what you mean by luck?" Here we have a real jewel. If you hired this idiot, you would have to spell everything out for them in the greatest detail.

Clearly, the best person, when asked if they are lucky, tells you they have had far more than their fair share of good luck. Next, you ask for two or three great examples. If these examples have the ring of truth, you should meet their salary demands and ask them when they can start working.

Keep a record of all the good luck stories you hear. That should be fun and give you a helpful frame of reference. Let me start your collection of examples of good luck with one I would use if you interviewed me. I was employed as a consultant to the Geneva, Switzerland, office of Caterpillar. On one of my trips, I went with three Cat executives to ski in the Swiss Alps. One of them had rented the chalet. The second person felt it was his job to do the cooking, and the Managing Director liked to do dishes! There wasn't much left for me to do but to enjoy my good fortune.

You may have the good fortune to interview two or more lucky people. It should be clear that whenever you find a lucky person, you should hire that person even if there is no job open. And if you only have one opening, but three qualified applicants, then the proper thing to do is immediately create jobs for the other two. Lucky people are in short supply.

THE MOST IMPORTANT APPLICATION OF THE METHOD

A blue ribbon, nonpartisan panel should be established by the Supreme Court. Any person who wanted to be elected president would have to undergo a thorough investigation by the FBI, who would document and substantiate their claims of being lucky. The panel would narrow down the list to five candidates whose names would be put on the ballot.

The Basic Communications Trauma

✦

(Why People Don't Tell the Truth)

In any country, any industry, any company, when you ask employees at all levels of the organization about critical organization problems, communications inevitably tops the list.

When senior management is told about the problem, they resolve to "fix" it with a multitude of initiatives. However, no matter how vigorous, determined, and creative the efforts of management are to correct communication problems, when you ask the same people the same question one year, three years, or five years later, the answer is the same—communications. The communication problems of organizations are *never* resolved.

So far, the root of this persistent and universal problem has eluded everyone, but this is your lucky day! You are about to learn the secret! You will find out not only the basic roots of all communication problems, but you will discover why a universally traumatic childhood experience determines whether people become economists, sales representatives, or politicians.

First, you must have a clear understanding of the foundation of effective communication. Effective communication is based on an honest exchange of information. It is impossible to have effective communication without an honest exchange. We all need to know the whole truth and nothing but the truth, but most people aren't consistently honest, candid, and truthful.

Let me give you two illustrations that prove my point.

151

You had a conversation with someone, perhaps as recently as last week, which lasted about an hour. After a half hour of discussion, the person leaned forward, in a somewhat conspiratorial tone, prefaced their next comment with this telling phrase: "To be perfectly honest with you," and then they were completely frank and open, for maybe three minutes.

They have just admitted that for the first half an hour they have been lying! They have just confessed they lie most of the time, and once in a while, they tell the truth!

As further proof of how honesty is uncommon, let me share some of my experiences with you. In the course of my career as a consultant, I have interviewed over ten thousand managers. A standard question during an employment interview is: "What are your strengths?"

In response to this question, more than ninety-five percent of interviewees will tell you that they are particularly good at getting along with people and that their interpersonal skills are simply outstanding. Is that a fact? Is that the truth? I don't think so. About thirty percent of these candidates have anticipated the question. They do not tell you the truth. They tell you what they think you want to hear. Another thirty percent suffer from delusions—they kid themselves. They do not tell you the truth because they lie to themselves. Another thirty percent know they have difficulty relating to others and just plain lie. A small percentage of all applicants are being honest when they tell you they get along well with others.

THE BASIC COMMUNICATIONS TRAUMA

The lack of honest and open communication is so widespread that it must be the result of some universal event impacting the lives of all people.

Freud felt that the defining event in peoples' lives was the Oedipal Complex. Freud was wrong. What really happened to us was that, one day when we were five or six years old, a friend of our parents visited our house for the first time. This friend was kind, thoughtful, warmhearted and had a great personality. Unfortunately, they had one ear missing, one crossed eye and a misshapen nose. When we saw this person, in the usually forthright and spontaneous way of children, we exclaimed, "Look at the ugly person!" Immediately, our mother or father turned red-faced, lost control, and meted out instant punishment. We were sent to our room or deprived of TV for three days, or perhaps severely punished.

We call this event and the ensuing reactions to it The Basic Communications Trauma. Since we are an acronym driven society, we will call it the BCT.

RESPONSES TO THE BCT

After having been physically and/or psychologically punished and sent to his room, the child has plenty of time to reflect on what has happened. The reactions of children vary tremendously. How they interpret this event dramatically and irrevocably influences them forever.

A small percentage of the population has an intensely violent reaction. They over-generalize and conclude that it is not safe to talk to people at all, and in fact, it's dangerous. **So, they make a lifelong decision to say as little as possible.** You know them. They tend to be shy and reticent. They always say the least during meetings, although they often may have the most to contribute.

Several centuries ago, a few of these people took a vow of silence and retreated to a monastery or convent for the rest of their lives. This reminds me of the joke about the woman who decided to join an order of nuns and took a vow of silence. One of the rules of the convent was that she was allowed to speak only two words every five years.

After the end of the first five years, she was ushered into the office of the mother superior. She said, "Food bad." At the end of the tenth year, when she had a chance to speak, she told the mother superior, "Bed hard". After fifteen years, when given the opportunity to say her two words, she said, "I quit!" Immediately, the mother superior said, *"That doesn't surprise me at all. Ever since you have been here, you have done nothing but complain."*

Another set of children makes a different decision. **They decide it is okay to talk, but that they will never tell the truth again.** What vocation do you think they select? You are right if you think they go into politics. They become what we normally call congenital or pathological liars. They lose the ability to distinguish between what is true and what is not.

The tradition of politicians avoiding the truth started with the father of our country, George Washington. It has recently come to light that his father beat the dickens out of George when he chopped down the cherry tree. But when he became an adult, an enterprising public relations consultant convinced him to put an entirely different spin on the story, and this led to the fable every school child learns about George saying, "I cannot tell a lie."

Another president of the United States decided to be quiet and also to be a politician. (Hard to imagine, isn't it?) His name was Calvin Coolidge. Once, a woman at dinner tried to coax him into talking. She said she had made a bet that she could get more than two words out of him. He said: "You lose."

The stringent avoidance of the truth reaches its epitome during the electoral season when the truth is totally disregarded. One presidential candidate, Adlai Stevenson, was one of the more witty people to grace the political scene. During one campaign, he said if his opponent stopped telling lies about him, *he would stop telling the truth about his opponent.*

A variation of the idea that it is not safe to tell the truth is **the idea that you can say something that is true about a person, as long as you don't say it directly to them**. As a result, it is a fairly universal pastime to talk about people behind their backs. However, when you are in the presence of someone, it is better to adopt the shopworn notion that if you can't say anything nice, then don't say anything at all.

Okay so far? As we continue, we are going to see that the BCT has a more significant impact on the vocational choices a person makes than any other factor. We will see that the BCT shapes the communication pattern of children for the rest of their lives. We will see that the permutations, combinations and variations of individualized responses to the BCT are staggering in their number, clearly showing the innate capacity of human beings to interpret the same kind of events in astonishingly different ways.

One of the most prevalent and least desirable responses to the BCT is: **don't say anything that makes sense.** In any meeting, the people who talk the most have the least to contribute. They talk a lot but say little. You find that there is an inverse relationship between the quantity and the quality of their contribution.

Despite this, these individuals feel that their comments are very profound. They will get a beatific expression on their face and come forth with some earth-shattering truism like, "We must make a profit." or "We have to look at costs." They expect all conversation to halt while everyone in the room absorbs such profundities. These people ignore the wisdom contained in a Chinese proverb: "Talk does not cook rice."

In my years as a trainer, I would work with a group of fifty or sixty people during a weeklong program on interpersonal competence. The participants were divided into seven or eight teams. As the week progressed, I would carefully monitor all the teams. On the final day of the program, I would take the two or three people from each team who monopolized the conversation with trite expressions and ask them to form two new teams.

Then all of the teams were given a competitive exercise. It is easy to imagine what happened. The teams composed of the big talkers came in last!

Another hallmark of these individuals is their command of all the latest buzzwords. This is best illustrated by the efforts of these people to assemble the maximum number of buzzwords into the currently popular no-organization-can-live-without-one mission statement.

On the next page you will see an example of such a statement.

WE WANT TO DEVELOP A STRATEGIC COMPETITIVE ADVANTAGE BY HAVING A GLOBALIZED VIEW OF CUSTOMER SATISFACTION BASED ON A WORLD CLASS DEDICATION TO TOTAL QUALITY, EMPHASIZING:

BENCHMARKING
REENGINEERING
VALUING DIVERSITY

IDENTIFYING CRITICAL SUCCESS FACTORS

AND

EMPOWERING
OUR PEOPLE TO UNDERGO A
PARADIGM SHIFT
IN THEIR CORE COMPETENCIES

It should be pointed out that the authors, who start out from the *"don't say anything that makes sense"* position, end up believing that what they said is not only sensible, but they think their profound statements should be etched in stone.

Another group believe the way to get ahead is to play the political game. They react to the BCT by a lifetime pursuit **of telling people in authority what they want to hear.** They decide when they were children that it wasn't good to make one's parents angry. They became determined to get on the good side of their parents. As they became adults, this shifted into a desire to appease the boss (i.e., a parent figure).

Next, we have the equivocators. There are always a few in any meeting. You know before the meeting has even started, that they will predictably flip-flop from one position to another. Their unconscious strategy is based on the notion *that* **if no one knows where they stand on an issue, they can avoid punishment.** Some of these individuals become scientists, and this is why all scientific papers predictably end with the conclusion that more research is needed.

Many of these people choose economics as a profession. George Bernard Shaw made the observation that if you laid all the economists in the world end-to-end, they still could not reach a conclusion. The widespread tendency of economists to give you a "on-the-one-hand, but on-the-other-hand" kind of answer prompted Harry Truman to make a statement that he would like to find "a one-armed economist."

What are the attributes of people who seek a career in sales? As very small children, they discovered that they had more fun playing with other kids and conning adults than they did playing by themselves with their toys. They are outgoing people whose endorphins are energized by personal contacts. The BCT, therefore, was especially unnerving for them, as it was a form of rejection.

In reflecting on their BCT predicament, it suddenly came to them that their mistake was spontaneity. They blurted out exactly what they thought. Their antidote? Instead of being spontaneous and telling the whole truth, the answer was not to be fully spontaneous but to be selective and **to *tell* part of the truth.**

The car salesman does not tell the prospective buyer that the car will lose half its value when driven off the lot. They do not mention any negatives. They stress the positive features, benefits, and advantages. Sales and marketing executives master the art of telling part of the truth and not getting caught. Their motto is: "If you can fool all of the people part of the time, or some of the people all of the time, go for it."

One of the healthier responses to the BCT is the acquisition of a pet. Why are most children animal lovers? Talking to animals is completely safe. The child can talk to the pet with no fear of repercussions. The pet remains totally loyal, always agrees with its mistress or master, and never talks back. In fact, this reaction to the BCT has a remarkably positive impact on both psychological and physical health. People with pets spend less time visiting doctors, are less likely to need psychiatric help and live longer.

In other cases, the child decides that it is not safe to talk; an entirely different tactic is used. This child decides to be an actor or actress. Why is that? When your job is to read the lines of a script you can never be held personally accountable for what you say.

By now, you have mastered the different types of reactions to the BCT. As you have seen, these reactions shape one's communication patterns, such as being quiet, never telling the truth, sticking with the facts, avoiding opinions, etc.

Let me turn to two of the more complex reactions to the BCT. Some children go to their room after having been punished. How do they react? They are happy, exhilarated, and fulfilled. These are the people who enjoy pain. They get psychic income from suffering. They become masochists.

For example, when they grow up they actually look forward to going to the dentist.

They develop a talent for saying the wrong thing at the wrong time to the wrong people. As a result, they are frequently rejected. The best of them could write a book on how to lose friends and alienate people. There is not one of us who at one time or another has not put our foot in our mouth accidentally and regretted it. The pain lovers, however, do it regularly and predictably.

In fact, I worked with one company that instituted an annual award for foot-in-mouth disease. The trophy was a bronzed shoe mounted on a nice platform, and it was presented to the person who had made the worst gaffe in the last year.

Diametrically opposed to the masochists are the children who determine that it is better to inflict pain than to receive it. They become sadists. In its mildest form, this is expressed in terms of the manager who gives ten criticisms for every one compliment. They get psychic income from making life miserable for their subordinates. You can easily detect people who suffer from the most serious form of this affliction. These people have a placard hanging on the wall in their office. It reads:

"Even though I have walked through the
Valley of the Shadow of Death,
I will fear no evil,
because I am the meanest sonofabitch in the Valley."

Many pain inflictors become dentists, IRS examiners, or they write computer instruction manuals. Perhaps the happiest pain inflictors find work in brokerage houses where they spend every day phoning customers who will need to come up with cash quickly to cover their margin calls.

I am sure there are some types or reactions to the BCT I have overlooked, but I hope we have discussed the more common varieties.

In summary, pet lovers have a complete feeling of security when they talk to their animals. Actors take no responsibility for reading their lines. Politicians swear they will never tell the truth. Gossips figure it is okay to tell the truth about Fred or Sally as long as they are talking to Sam or Jane. The quiet people take refuge in silence; the loudmouths talk a lot but say nothing. Equivocators straddle all the issues. Sales and marketing people make a living from telling partial truths.

Some people like pain and some people prefer to make others suffer. Do these people change? Does a leopard change its spots? Trying to help some people overcome these lifelong patterns of communicating is like teaching a pig how to sing. It is a waste of time, and it annoys the pig.

THE ELITE MINORITY

I realize that you are different. How do I know you are an exception? I could almost hear you chuckle as you read about the different types and the compellingly accurate descriptions of people in your family and in your organization. But you were saying to yourself as you read each description, "That's true, but it doesn't apply to me." You are honest, candid, and tell the truth consistently. As you obviously have continued to read this material, you must have a good sense of humor. It is easy to surmise from the above that you are probably very attractive, highly intelligent, a good judge of character, and have tremendous insight into yourself. You were able to overcome the BCT.

What was your secret? You didn't over-generalize. While other people decided, based on a single event, that they would never tell the truth, you avoided that trap. Instead, when you were punished for speaking your mind as a child, you were able to look at the situation objectively. You concluded that whenever you had embarrassed your mother or father in public, you got into trouble. So, since that time you have followed one simple rule:

Never embarrass your parents (or parental figures like bosses) in public, but, aside from that, honesty is the best policy.

Why is honesty the best policy? The founder of Motorola said the real reason you should be honest is that people are going to find out the truth sooner or later.

You are one of the few who were able to get through childhood without the BCT changing your lifelong style of communication. You and people like you are rare indeed, and we must stick together.

About the Author

Dr. Glasscock has been an independent management consultant for fifty years and has had the opportunity to learn from some extraordinarily talented people. This book is a way to pass on what he's learned from them.

Dr. Glasscock has worked with people from all organizational levels and functional areas: research, finance, manufacturing, marketing, human resources, sales, engineering, and general management. He's worked with folks in many different businesses: people making railroad cars, toys, pharmaceutical products, guns, airplanes, heavy construction equipment, metals, and chemicals. He's consulted with real estate developers, bankers, brokers, managers of gaming casinos, and directors of the IRS. For forty years, Dr. Glasscock has also traveled to Europe, working with a broad spectrum of European managers.

He has interviewed more than 10,000 executives as part of an effort to determine the talent pool of the organization or as part of the pre-employment process. He's conducted intensive, one-week training sessions on leadership for 3,000 managers from more than 200 companies. He was Adjunct Professor of Cornell University's School of Industrial and Labor

Relations and served as a member of the Board of Directors of Primex Technologies.

Dr. Glasscock grew up in Kansas City, Missouri, and received a PhD in Clinical Psychology from Washington University at St. Louis. He was first in his class. His address is ed@edglasscock.com.

Acknowledgements

My biggest debt is to my family. My daughter, Jenna, made significant contributions to every chapter. The computer skills of my son Tom and his wife Ellen proved to be invaluable. Most of all, my wife, Mariben, stood by me all the way, designed the cover, and corrected innumerable mistakes on every page.

I am also especially indebted to those who helped take the book up to a new level: Diana Bacci, Leslie Bell, Chris D'Amato and his wife Grey Valenti, Bob Goodpasture, Jack Grebb, M.D., and Kassy McCourty.

Finally, to the many individuals who critiqued chapters and/or who have taught me so much.

Carol Aloisi, Al Altomari, Jeff Bailey Val Brunell, Bill Clemens, Ann Clinton, Bill Cordivari, Bob Croce, Barbara Crosby, Bill Curnow, Robert Del Femine, Doug DeMaire, Peter DiLullo, Eric Eichler, Jeanne Fedoryk, Seth Fischer, John Johnson, Mike Kafrissen, M.D., JimKahn, M.D., Bob Kavesh,Ph.D., Mark Klausner, M.D., Frank Konings, Ph.D., Wanda Hope, Dave Marvel, Deepak Massand, John McGuire, Ph.D., Eric Milledge, Lynn (The Trouble Maker) MorganBork, Paul Motheral, Scott Myers, Michael Paulik, Michelle Paulik, Ludo Peeters, John Reardon, Eileen Roan, Ed Ruhe, Joe Rupp, Nauman Shah, Mike Sinclair, Tom Spalding, Peter Tattle, Dale Turnbull, Janet Vergis, Tom Watson, Fos Whitlock, Bill Youngster, Yvonne Zazzara-Krysztow

0-595-33415-6

Printed in the United Kingdom
by Lightning Source UK Ltd.
104246UKS00001B/232-234